"Syracuse's Enterprises"
by Joseph A. Porcello

Produced in cooperation with the
Greater Syracuse Chamber of Commerce

Windsor Publications, Inc.
Northridge, California

SYRACUSE

THE HEART OF NEW YORK

ALEXIS O'NEILL

with contributions by Joseph A. Porcello

Windsor Publications, Inc.—History Books
Division

Managing Editor: Karen Story
Design Director: Alexander d'Anca

Staff for *Syracuse: The Heart of New York*
Manuscript Editor: Kevin Taylor
Photo Editor: Laura Cordova
Copy Editor: Melanie J. Eichel
Editor, Corporate Profiles: Brenda Berryhill
Production Editor, Corporate Profiles: Phyllis
    Gray
Senior Proofreader: Susan J. Muhler
Editorial Assistants: Didier Beauvoir, Thelma
    Fleischer, Kim Kievman, Rebecca Kropp,
    Michael Nugwynne, Kathy B. Peyser, Pat
    Pittman, Theresa J. Solis
Publisher's Representative, Corporate Profiles:
    Rob Ottenheimer
Layout Artist, Corporate Profiles: Mari Catherine
    Preimesberger
Designer: Thomas McTighe

Library of Congress Cataloging-in-Publication
Data
O'Neill, Alexis, 1949—
    Syracuse: the heart of New York/Alexis
    O'Neill with Joseph A. Porcello.—1st ed.
        p. 256 cm. 23 x 31
    "Published in cooperation with the Greater
Syracuse Chamber of Commerce."
    Bibliography: p. 251
    Includes index.
    ISBN 0-89781-275-1
    1. Syracuse (N.Y.)—Economic
conditions.   2. Syracuse (N.Y.)—Economic
conditions—Pictorial works.   I. Porcello,
Joseph A.   II. Greater Syracuse Chamber of
Commerce.   III. Title.
HC108.S95054   1988
330.9747'66043—dc19   88-27866
                                            CIP
ISBN: 0-89781-275-1

Windsor Publications, Inc.
Elliot Martin, Chairman of the Board
James L. Fish III, Chief Operating Officer

Previous page: Bright lights of
Syracuse. Photo by Oliver
McConnell Photography, Inc.

To Meredith "Ede" Estoff —whose love of Syracuse was contagious

The sun sets over Montezuma Wildlife Refuge. Photo by Dan Vecchio.

Contents

Acknowledgments

I would like to thank Jeff Unaitis of the Greater Syracuse Chamber of Commerce for his professional support and welcome enthusiasm throughout this project; David Boesaar for his continued encouragement; and the countless leaders and librarians in Central New York for their invaluable assistance during the research process, and for their counsel, guidance, and advice as the manuscript took shape.

Thanks to the works of glaciers long ago, waterfalls abound in the Greater Syracuse area. Photo by Dan Vecchio

Prologue

As the Greater Syracuse Chamber of Commerce celebrates its centennial during 1989, we are encouraged to reflect on the many changes and challenges that this community has faced during the past century.

From its beginnings as a meeting place for several Indian nations and a marshy settlement in the wilderness, to its reputation as the "Queen of the Sister Cities" that developed along the Erie Canal, to a thriving industrial town that emerged from both the Depression and World War II even stronger than before, to the "Heart of New York" that appeals to new residents and visitors alike: Syracuse has met each and every challenge that the future has held for it.

As we enter a new century and a new era that some have called the "age of the entrepreneur," it is indeed reassuring to recognize that Greater Syracuse is again prepared for the challenges offered by an increasingly complex global community.

The Chamber and the participating firms whose success stories are shared here are sponsoring the publication of *Syracuse: The Heart of New York* to help the community recognize the dramatic ways in which business and industry can and should strive to foster civic improvements that benefit the welfare of everybody who calls Greater Syracuse home.

We think this book captures the essence of the entrepreneurial spirit that has brought Syracuse this far, and will propel us well into the twenty-first century.

Harry E. Goetzmann, Jr.
Chairman
Greater Syracuse Chamber of Commerce

(Mr. Goetzmann serves as chairman of the Greater Syracuse Chamber of Commerce for 1988-1989. He is president of Continental Information Systems Corp.)

Previous page: The sun rises
above these barns. Photo by Dan
Vecchio

Part One

Two Centuries of Progress

Ice skaters gather at Erie Canal at
Clinton Square for a favorite winter pastime in this early 1900s
scene. Courtesy, Onondaga
County Savings Bank

Chapter One

Looking Back
A Tradition of Innovation and Prosperity

by Alexis O'Neill

Boisterous, rowdy salt-boilers rocked the tavern with earthy merrymaking as the journalist from downstate New York struggled to write his impressions of a crossroads that claimed to be a village. A village! On that crisp October morning in 1820, the journalist, W.L. Stone, saw a few houses standing upon low, marshy ground, with a tangle of thickets and trees surrounding the simple wooden structures.

A man possessed by a dream, Joshua Forman, tried to convince the journalist that this village would become a formidable city. "Mr. Forman," said Stone, turning to his companion, "do you call this a village? It would make an owl weep to fly over it."

"Never mind," Forman replied, "you will live to see it a city yet." And he did.

Some might call it the luck of geography. After all, the center is the center, no matter how you slice up a state. But it takes more than just the natural lay of the land to create a region so deserving of its appellations that it is hard to be a skeptic. Appellations such as Keeper of the Central Fire. Crossroads of the Empire State. Heart of New York. For Greater Syracuse these appellations are perfectly fitting, and skeptics have to look elsewhere for a target. More than luck has turned a region rich in natural resources into a vibrant, dynamic city.

Vision pulled five warring Iroquois nations together to make one peaceable kingdom—earning Syracuse distinction as Keeper of the Central Fire. Vision took a swamp and turned it into a canal, and saw the sense of two intersecting paths and cre-

Dressed in traditional dress of the Onondaga Nation, Tracy Thomas wears a *qus-to-weh*, or headdress, which incorporates the design of the Hiawatha Wampum Belt. The central figures represent the original five nations of the confederacy. Photo by Larry McKenzie

Known as the Hondinonshonni, these early inhabitants spread throughout Central New York State. The Iroquois nations, as they were named by French explorers in later years, quarreled and warred among themselves. Social order broke down while blood feuds, hunger, and cannibalism reigned. Enemies of the Iroquois relentlessly attacked them.

Into this turmoil came the Peace Maker—a Huron Indian who preached a message of peace, reason, law, and the abolishment of war. He invited the Iroquois people to unite in a confederacy under one law. With Hayentwatha (Hiawatha) as spokesman, these two men convinced four of the Iroquois nations to join them: the Mohawk, Oneida, Cayuga, and Seneca. Yet there was one holdout: the Onondaga. Situated on the eastern shore of Onondaga Lake near the present site of Syracuse, the Onondagas were at the center of all the nations, with the Cayugas and Senecas to the west, and the Oneidas and Mohawks to the east. The Onondagas' leader, Tohdadaho, was a skillful politician who ruled and maintained power through fear. Overwhelmed by the political and military skill of Peace Maker, Hayentwatha, and the chiefs of the four nations, Tohdadaho ultimately agreed to join them.

Resulting from this union was the Great

Law, which codified the entire structure of the Five Nations government (later to become Six Nations with the addition of the Tuscaroras). So encompassing was the Great Law that many believe that the Constitution of the United States was based upon it.

The "capital" of the Iroquois government was—and still is—at Syracuse, where the original Tree of Peace was planted. Weapons of war were buried beneath it. There, representatives of the Grand Council still meet and take action based on unanimous decisions. Syracuse continues to maintain its tradition as Keeper of the Council Fire.

THE FRENCH

As early as the 1600s French explorers and missionaries recognized the political and economic importance of the Syracuse region and began to venture into the Onondaga country. Samuel Champlain made a futile attempt in 1615 to defeat the Onondagas. He built a tower by the palisades of their longhouse village, thought to be at the site of the present-day oil terminal storage area on the shore of Onondaga Lake, and attacked the villagers with firearms. After being seriously wounded, Champlain was carried back to Canada in a basket, earning a dubious reputation for being the first to introduce firearms to the Iroquois.

Conditions were more pleasant in 1654 when a Jesuit missionary, Father Simon Le Moyne, was invited by the Onondagas to establish a mission in the heart of their territory. Gannentaha (now Onondaga Lake) was a practical site, for it could be reached from Quebec City by water routes and was near the village where the Iroquois Grand Council met.

But the mission, Sainte Marie de Gannentaha, was not destined to survive. Not all of the Five Nations agreed with this attempt to make peace with the French or accepted the presence of this fortified mission within their homeland. Fearing a sudden shift in sentiment, the French staged an ingenious evacuation of Sainte Marie. They hosted a feast on March 20, 1658, to which they invited their Indian neighbors. When the revelers grew drowsy from celebrating, the French paddled away in the dark. They never again attempted to establish a permanent settlement on Iroquois lands.

Out of this experience, however, came a discovery that was to change Syracuse forever. During his visit in 1654, Father Le Moyne sampled water from a spring by Onondaga Lake. Surprised by its salty taste, he collected some of the brine in a kettle and boiled it. The result was the first production of salt in what was to become Onondaga County.

What Le Moyne could not guess at the time was that the entire Syracuse region was phenomenally rich in salt deposits—rich enough to put Syracuse on the map as the only place in the continental United States that produced salt commercially; rich enough to earn Syracuse its reputation as the Salt City. It took more than 100 years for the salt deposits to be rediscovered and worked commercially, but when they were, the financial benefits were felt not only by the local settlers but by the entire state of New York.

Below: Chief Tohdadaho, a despotic, snake-haired Onondagan was the last to accept Peace Maker's teachings. With his acceptance of the Great Law came the Great Peace among the Hoinonshonni. Courtesy, Onondaga County Savings Bank

Bottom: This is artist Richard Hill's watercolor of "Orthodox Onondaga."

Harvesting salt from solar vats was once a common sight in the "Salt City." Courtesy, Onondaga County Savings Bank

THE START OF THE SALT INDUSTRY

In colonial times salt was in high demand as a food preservative. The bulk of the salt used in the colonies was transported by ship from Turks Island in the Bahamas. When Great Britain cut off the Bahamian trade with America in 1789, a new supply source was crucial.

The salt industry in Syracuse began slowly. It was not until 1788 that the salt springs were rediscovered. After the Revolutionary War, veterans Asa Danforth and Comfort Tyler moved to Onondaga at the invitation of local trader and Revolutionary War hero Ephraim Webster. As the story goes, the men, low on salt, went with cup in hand to an Onondaga Indian neighbor to borrow a few of the precious grains. Not only did the neighbor fill their request, but he took the men to the same spring from which Le Moyne had taken a drink over 100 years earlier.

Danforth and Tyler later pounded two forked stakes into the ground and hung a black kettle from a crossbar. They filled the kettle with brine and within nine hours had boiled down about 30 pounds of salt. No more borrowing for them. Now they could preserve all the fish and game they needed for their families.

Nathaniel Loomis improved upon a good plan. He spearheaded the commercial production of salt when he introduced large iron cauldrons set in a stone arch in 1793. With several fires blazing at once, the output dramatically increased.

The State of New York was quick to see salt as a revenue source, and in 1795 it assumed full control over the salt lands. Stone arches were replaced with salt blocks, which consisted of 50 or 60 kettles in parallel rows within one building. These salt blocks were owned by individual businessmen. From the 1700s up to 1908, the land around Onondaga Lake was owned by the State of New York and called the Salt Springs Reservation. From scores of wells sunk along the southern shore of Onondaga Lake, state-owned pumphouses collected brine and pumped it to the salt blocks. Between 1797 and 1800, 50,000 bushels of salt were produced per year. The figure doubled shortly after that.

For many years salt was the primary industry in the area, and Syracuse was the only place on the American continent that produced it commercially. Since money was scarce, salt was also the staple of barter. One bushel of salt, which sold for 25 cents, was worth two pounds of ham or pork, two bushels of oats, eight and a half pounds of meal, or a quarter bushel of corn.

Harvesting salt was considerably easier than shipping it out of the area, however. Wagons and canoes were the prime means of transportation. Shipping a load of salt to Pittsburgh—a regular destination—took well over a week at best. Boats had to use the unpredictable natural waterways, and wagons had to traverse the rough and dangerous roadways. As a result of these difficulties, salt prices could be driven as high as $6.50 a bushel—more than two dozen times the price at the point of origin.

BUILDING THE ERIE CANAL

In the early years of the nineteenth century, Syracuse was little more than a swamp. Sixty new settlers, most of whom were involved in the nascent salt industry, had arrived in the region by 1803. Two mills, a tavern, one frame house, and the swamp were all that marked what was to become the city.

But one settler, Joshua Forman, so strongly believed Syracuse would be a great city that he built his home and business on the swamp near the crossing of two Iroquois paths. To the north was an established salt-producing settlement at Salina, and to the south was a farming community at Onondaga, but the lowlands of Syracuse were thought by many to be useless and unhealthy. Yet visions of prosperity guided Forman. A judge, he was elected to the state legislature in 1807 on the Canal platform.

The idea of creating a peaceful waterway extending from the Hudson to the Great Lakes had first been proposed by Gouverneur Morris, a member of the First Continental Congress, in 1777. As the tide of emigration flowed westward after the Revolutionary War, the idea of an inland waterway captured the imaginations of politicians, planners, and producers. Salt makers were eager to find an economical way to ship their goods.

Forman was among those who championed Morris' cause. By 1808 he had secured the passage of a joint resolution calling for a survey of proposed routes. And what better place to run a canal than through Syracuse's low, flat land? Interestingly, the choice for the task of surveying the canal route was Syracusan James Geddes. A pioneer in the salt industry, Geddes was also a leading activist for what he saw as a perfect solution to the industry's transportation problem.

Geddes, a man of many talents and concerns, was a former member of Congress and had served in the New York State Legislature twice. From his position of power he had pushed for the building of the Erie Canal, arguing it would serve not only the salt industry but also the other growing agricultural and business interests of the state. Although he had retired from politics by 1809, this schoolteacher, salt manufacturer, politician, lawyer, and land surveyor was invited to lay out the 363-mile route of the canal. Using the simplest of equipment, men then began to clear the seemingly impenetrable wilderness—a task that President Thomas Jefferson had dismissed as "a little short of madness." Due to Forman's endeavors, Onondaga Lake was lowered by two feet and the swamps were drained.

The Erie Canal's route followed a course through what eventually became downtown Syracuse, a mere stone's throw away from Forman's home, and the swamp became a center of commerce and was named Clinton

Getting the water from Lake Shore over a 19-mile, hill-and-dale trip to Syracuse was a major accomplishment in the 1890s. A gravity-flow system, where no pumps were required, was used. Courtesy, Onondaga County Savings Bank

Primo Carinera, the "World's strongest man," is seen here in a heavyweight bout in Syracuse. Courtesy, John Dowling

Square. Syracuse's population exploded. In 1820 the population of Syracuse numbered 250. By the time the Erie Canal had opened statewide in 1825, the town's population had jumped to 600. Five years later, when the canal was being enlarged, more than 11,000 people were living in Syracuse.

The building of the Erie Canal may have been America's first lesson in civil engineering. Men learned their trade on the job as they cleared the land, dug a 40-foot-wide ditch, and built 83 locks, 300 bridges, and 18 aqueducts.

As portions of the canal were completed, they were immediately put to use. In 1820, 73 new canal boats left Syracuse in a parade to mark the completion of nearly all the middle section. When the full length of the Erie Canal was completed in 1825, Governor De Witt Clinton traveled with the inaugural Buffalo-to-New-York flotilla, accompanied by a tremendous celebration. As Clinton boarded the flag-draped *Seneca Chief* on October 26, a cannon roared a salute from a nearby hill. Cannons all along the route repeated this salute in tandem. Eighty-one minutes later, a response reached

the *Seneca Chief* and the procession began. At Sandy Hook on November 2, 1825, the historic "Wedding of the Waters" was carried out. Clinton poured a keg of water from Lake Erie into the ocean as a symbol that the Great Lakes and the Atlantic Ocean were now united.

Syracusans had much to celebrate. At last there was an inexpensive means of transporting their precious "white gold" to market. Freight rates from Buffalo to New York City dropped from $100 a ton to $12 a ton. The price of salt dropped from $60 a barrel to $6 a barrel. Travel from Albany to Buffalo, which had taken six weeks by stagecoach, took only six days by canal.

A NEW PROSPERITY

With increased opportunity, the population of Syracuse jumped 282 percent between 1820 and 1830, and the vigorous beginnings of an inland industrial center were established. By 1848 Syracuse had been incorporated as a city.

Transportation opportunities provided by the canal and Syracuse's central location in the state attracted new businesses, including Onondaga Pottery Company (later Syracuse China Corporation), Solvay Process (later a division of Allied Chemical), and so many breweries that Syracuse grew to become one of the largest beer producing centers in the United States, second only to New York City. Today Anheuser-Busch and Miller Brewing carry on the beer-making tradition in Central New York.

Between 1830 and 1840 banks sprouted like mushrooms after a rain. The first bank in Syracuse was the Onondaga County Bank, which began in 1830 with $150,000 in capital stock. The Oswego Canal, which led to Lake Ontario, met with the Erie Canal one block east of Clinton Square in downtown Syracuse. At this juncture all cargo-carrying boats were weighed at the Syracuse Weighlock Building and charged a toll. Because New York State had a policy of depositing tolls collected in the area into local banks, financial institutions flourished. The steady flow of cash enabled banks to loan money for the formation of new businesses and the expansion of existing ones. With the development of shipping, warehousing, retail, and wholesale business trade, Syracuse became a center of commerce in upstate

This view of South Salina Street in the 1850s shows some of the buildings in this downtown rail hub. On the left is the Syracuse House replaced later by the Onondaga Savings Bank Building and Vanderbilt Center. In the distance is the spire of the First Presbyterian Church. Courtesy, Onondaga County Savings Bank

New York. Although many of the banks had short lives, several banks that opened during the canal era are still thriving today. They include Key Bank, which can be traced back to the Bank of Salina, opened in 1832; Merchants Bank (1850), which is Syracuse's oldest commercial bank in terms of continuous service; and Onondaga County Savings Bank (1855). Until its purchase by Norstar Bank in 1987, Syracuse Savings Bank (1849) was the community's oldest commercial/savings institution.

A richly textured lifestyle was inspired by the Erie Canal. Through Syracuse came floating vaudeville shows, libraries, museums, missionaries striving to save souls, and circus performers. Syracuse society people built homes where they could be seen from the canal. The first fashionable addresses were on West and East Water streets, and when Moses Burnet moved to James Street, it was a source of pride that his mansion, completed in 1842 for the shocking sum of $20,000, boasted a view of passing canal boats. In 1857 *Appleton's Handbook for American Travel* described Syracuse as "a large and elegant city, with a population of over 26,000."

"Playing Syracuse" was a given for the foremost stage and opera stars from the late 1840s onward. In 1848 a former Baptist church hosted *Uncle Tom's Cabin*, an appropriate choice for a city that was soon to become a hotbed of abolitionist fervor. P.T. Barnum introduced Jenny Lind to her adoring fans, and Charles Dickens, Sarah Bernhardt, and Edwin Booth walked the boards of the Weiting Opera House. Buffalo Bill Cody skyrocketed to fame in Syracuse when he created the precursor to his famous Wild West shows by ignoring the tame opening of *Scouts of the Prairie* and starting with a shooting scene instead.

The Erie Canal was a prime route for immigrants traveling westward. From 1820 to 1860, one-fourth of all U.S. population growth was due to European immigration. Two-thirds of the immigrants entered America through the Port of New York; of those landing in New York City in 1855, one-third listed New York State as their final destination. In the mid-nineteenth century most of the immigrants came from Germany and Ireland. In Germany, overpopulation and the burdensome feudal obligations laid upon farmers caused people to migrate, and in Ireland the great famine inspired many to seek a new life in America. By the 1830s opportunities for work were plentiful in Syracuse, for the Erie Canal was being enlarged and railroads were being built. Large groups of German and Irish immigrants settled here, bringing distinctive cultural heritages to the growing city.

GROWTH AND CHANGE

By 1850 the wood supply that had fueled the salt blocks in earlier years was exhausted. Salt manufacturers turned to coal for fuel. Because the coal had to be shipped up from Pennsylvania on the Chenango Canal, the cost of coal boosted the price of salt. This led salt manufacturers to employ a cheaper form of energy to evaporate the brine. The solution came in the form of the sun's rays. Brine was pumped into a series of shallow vats where it was left to evaporate by the sun and wind. Every few weeks the salt crop was planted, and the crop was staggered so that harvesting went on continuously. Each solar vat had a movable cover which was mounted on rollers. At any sign of rain, the saltwater boss clanged an alarm bell. Workers and their families raced to the salt fields to pull these protective covers over the salt crop.

Syracuse exported salt worldwide throughout most of the nineteenth century. In 1862, the salt trade's peak year, more than 9 million bushels were produced, primarily in response to a blockade against foreign salt during the Civil War.

By the 1860s the railroad industry was making an impression on Syracuse. It wooed passengers and, eventually, shippers away from the canal with fulfilled promises of speed, cleanliness, and convenience.

Some railroad travelers only stopped in Syracuse on their way to other destinations, while others came to spend some time in the city. During the 1870s and 1880s Syracuse earned a reputation as a convention city, becoming the center for many political gatherings.

Hotel business boomed. By 1867, 27 hotels catered to travelers. The most elaborate was the Hotel Vanderbilt. Commodore Cornelius Vanderbilt presented the hotel with an oil portrait of himself, and also spent one night of his second honeymoon there. The Syracuse House, on the corner of Salina and Genesee streets, hosted many famous visitors, including John Quincy Adams, Martin Van Buren, Millard Fillmore, Henry Clay, Daniel Webster, Horace Greeley, and Charles Dickens.

A common sight was that of runners clanging bells at the depots, touting the fine features of their respective hotel dining rooms and even urging passengers on 30-minute stopovers to enjoy a feast before moving on. The Globe Hotel on Salina, the St. Charles in the University Building, and the Citizen's Coffee House and Ice Cream Saloon competed daily for patrons.

In spite of the dominance of the salt industry during the nineteenth century, Syracuse never became a one-industry city. Unlike cities that specialized in one major product, Syracuse earned a reputation for being one of the most diversified manufacturing cities in the country. When the salt business went into a decline after the Civil War, businesses related to it made adaptations characteristic of Syracusans' enterprising spirit.

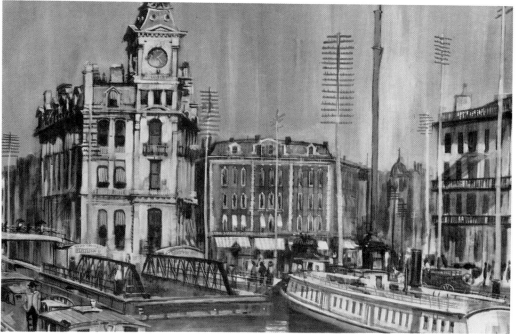

Above: This street scene was typical of the late 1800s. Courtesy, John Dowling

This 1890s scene shows canal boats gliding to and from Clinton Square. A landmark for canal travelers was the famous Town Clock, center. Shakespeare Hall also stands in the center. To the right is the Syracuse House and in the foreground is the Liberty Pole. Lithograph by Onondaga County Savings Bank

Highways, waterways, railways, and airways comprise the highly successful transportation network that keeps Syracuse in touch with the world. Photo by John Dowling

Chapter Two

Connecting the Community

Transportation and Distribution

by Alexis O'Neill

With double-edged, solid iron blades reaching up to eight feet in front and movable blades on both sides, the machine looks like something from another planet. On top a yellow light flashes. White spotlights beam on the sides. Snow has fallen during the night, and 53 Onondaga County plows have been doing double duty making sure roads are clear and ready for morning commuters.

Dawn comes, and semis laden with goods pull out onto Syracuse's network of highways. Commuters tune their radios to WSYR or WHEN to catch traffic updates from Al Verley and Captain Scott King. CENTRO buses speed passengers to their destinations, and downtown trolleys drop off workers and shoppers at strategic locations throughout the heart of the city. Although snow is in the air, throngs of coatless, bootless people bustle across the spans of the skybridges which connect major portions of Syracuse's commercial center.

Another day has begun. Syracuse is on the move.

Ease of movement characterizes city traffic throughout the day, in every season. Syracusans' vigorous lifestyle has spawned a transportation network surpassed by few in the country. Located literally at the crossroads of New York State, Greater Syracuse is one of the leading distribution centers in the Northeast. Highways, waterways, railways, and airways connect more than 63 million people within a 300-mile radius of Syracuse,

The highway system in Greater Syracuse provides fast and efficient routes. The maximum commuting time for most residents is 20 minutes. Photo by Dan Vecchio

central meeting point for transportation systems. Paths worn wide by the people of the Iroquois nations as they traveled to hunting grounds and longhouse villages became prime routes for new settlers in their westward travels. The city of Syracuse grew where the Great Genesee Road crossed the Seneca Turnpike. Corduroy roads gave way to the first plank road in the country as settlers tried to find more efficient ways to transport Syracuse's products to wider markets.

Today two major interstate highways intersect at Syracuse: Interstate 81, which runs north-south, and the New York State Thruway (Interstate 90), which runs east-west. For motor carriers, next-day delivery is the rule—including shipments traveling up to 500 miles away.

The New York State Thruway runs closer to Syracuse than to most cities along its 440-mile route, and it serves the area with six interchanges. When the Thruway first opened in 1954, industries, jobs, and housing exploded with activity. Linking major urban centers from New York City to Buffalo, the Thruway joins with other highways that lead to Connecticut and the Mid-Atlantic states. Just below Albany the Berkshire section of the thruway continues east into the Massachusetts Turnpike, which terminates in Boston. At the western end the Thruway joins with other interstate routes, providing express service to Chicago and the far West.

Beginning at the Canadian border at the Thousand Island Bridge, Interstate 81 provides uninterrupted travel through Syracuse to Cortland and on to the southern border of New York State. From there I-81 continues through Pennsylvania to Tennessee, with connections to Baltimore and Washington.

Greater Syracuse's highway system not only provides fast and efficient routes in and out of the region, but facilitates commuter travel as well. The maximum commuting time for most residents is 20 minutes. Two major routes provide access to the city and surrounding towns. Interstate 690 begins at Exit 39 of the Thruway, near the New York State Fairgrounds. From there it runs east through Syracuse, connecting with I-481 near East Syracuse. Interstate 481, which intersects I-81 both north and south of Syracuse, forms a beltway around the city and provides direct access to Fulton through its northern extension.

linking the populations of Boston, New York, Philadelphia, Baltimore, Pittsburgh, Toronto, and Montreal. Other major markets lie within 400 to 500 miles, making efficient shipment of goods, close customer contact, and minimal freight charges a possibility. The sophistication of transportation facilities for commercial and other uses helped to earn Syracuse 14th place among the 329 metropolitan areas examined in the second edition of Rand McNally's *Places Rated Almanac*.

HIGHWAYS

From its earliest days Syracuse has been a

Syracuse is well established as a warehousing and distribution center. More than 150 trucking companies, including 11 of the nation's top 12 common carriers of general freight, service the Greater Syracuse area, as do local trucking firms. United Parcel Service, Roadway, Yellow Freight System, Consolidated Freightways, Ryder/PIE Nationwide, Overnight Transport, ABF Freight Systems, Carolina Freight Carriers, Smith's Transfer, Transcon Lines, and Preston Trucking all transport goods from and to Syracuse. Located at the new Thruway Exit 39 in the town of Van Buren is the Interstate Island Industrial Park, which offers even more potential for growth in warehousing capabilities.

Regional carriers, some of which are locally owned and operated, provide service within the northeast quadrant of the United States. Other carriers carry freight only within New York State or specialize in local pickups and deliveries. Still others facilitate the transportation of goods to port cities, where goods are transferred to ships for transport to international markets. Customer service and rate flexibility are areas that have benefited from the deregulation of the motor carrier industry. Discount plans are offered by the rate bureaus and the individual carriers. Inbound and outbound shipments may be covered by these discount plans, which are available to both small and large volume shippers. Shipping associations, local agents, and brokers provide assistance with cost-management techniques.

WATERWAYS

Although water routes brought trappers and missionaries from Canada to the Syracuse region in the 1600s, it was not until the Erie Canal was finished in 1825 that water became the primary means of transportation for goods and passengers. For almost a century the Erie Canal dominated regional transportation. This 363-mile route connected the Port of New York and the Hudson River in the east with Buffalo, Lake Erie, and the other Great Lakes in the west. The Erie Canal reduced transportation time between Albany and Buffalo from six weeks to six days.

Not only was Syracuse along the popular east-west Erie Canal route, it was also the termination point for the Oswego Canal, which provided a direct route to Lake On-

tario. It is not surprising that Syracuse emerged as the manufacturing and transportation center of the Northeast in the 1800s. Immigrants traveling along the canal entered the work force, and businesses flourished.

With the construction of the Barge Canal System in 1917, the route of the Erie Canal moved north of the city and no longer ran through downtown's Clinton Square. Because the Syracuse portion of the Erie Canal was filled in and paved over to become Erie Boulevard, many hold the mistaken notion that the canal days are over. Yet water routes continue to carry millions of tons of freight through New York State to major ports each year. While the original and enlarged Erie Canal depended on mules and

Water routes carry millions of tons of freight through New York State to major ports each year. Photo by John Dowling

horses to pull barges along, modern engine-powered barges make use of New York State's natural waterways to transport goods.

Today Syracuse is convenient to several of America's major East Coast ports. New York City and Philadelphia are approximately 250 miles away, while Boston and Baltimore are approximately 300 miles away. Low-cost connections can be made between Syracuse and these ports in a day or less, and some Syracuse carriers specialize in the shipment and transfer of containerized freight into oceangoing vessels.

Located 34 miles from Syracuse on the southeast shore of Lake Ontario is Central New York's own deep-water port, the Port of Oswego. It is the first major port of call on the Great Lakes, and it offers direct service to all major ports in the free world. Strategically located 45 minutes from the entrance of the St. Lawrence River, this port provides important access to the St. Lawrence Seaway, a network of waters and locks connecting the Great Lakes with Montreal, Canada, via the St. Lawrence River. From Montreal, the St. Lawrence carries oceangoing vessels through to the Atlantic Ocean.

Approximately 1.5 million tons of bulk and general cargo are handled annually at the Port of Oswego. The east-side terminal can dock ships with drafts of up to 28 feet along a 1,900-foot wharf. Storage facilities include a sprinkler-protected transit building for general cargo, two bulk storage warehouses, and open storage space. The west-side terminal has a 1,000-foot-long pier, a one-million-bushel grain elevator, and 28,000 square feet of covered storage.

The Port of Oswego is easily reached by rail, highway, or the New York State Barge Canal System. During a recent season it handled 599,356 net tons of cargo, with an economic impact of $14,915,340 in benefits for the community. An ongoing $6 million expansion project, begun in 1984, underscores the importance of the Port of Oswego to the Central New York transportation network.

Oswego is only one of the many ports connected by the New York State Barge Canal System. Other ports served by this vital inland waterway include those along Lake Champlain, the Hudson River, and the Eastern Seaboard. This toll-free system is 524 miles long. The barge canal mainline runs east-west across New York and comprises the contemporary Erie Canal. From the Hudson River near Albany to the Niagara River near Buffalo, it still follows the general path of the industry-building Erie Canal of the 1800s. One sideline connects the current Erie Canal with Onondaga Lake and the Onondaga Lake Terminal in Syracuse, and another connects the Erie with the Port of Oswego.

Maintained to a depth of 14 feet from Oswego to Albany—a section also referred to as the Great Lakes-Hudson River Waterway—the canal provides economical transportation for bulk items such as petroleum, coal, and chemicals. Pleasure boats account for a growing volume of traffic each year during the canal's April-to-November season.

RAILWAYS

Since the arrival of the first steam train in Syracuse in 1839, transportation opportunities in this region have been broadened. Shrewd planners laid rail parallel to the Erie Canal, and thus began a century of competition between the land and water routes. Tracks ran down the middle of city streets, and as many as 100 trains were passing through Syracuse in a single day.

Although the railroads were an appreciated—and necessary—service, the citizens of Syracuse grew impatient with the steady flow of trains through the city. There were long delays at the 29 grade crossings, office buildings were being covered with gritty soot, and Syracuse became the butt of many vaudeville jokes as "the city with trains in the streets." With the growing popularity of automobiles, there came a growing cry to construct an elevated route for trains.

The Port of Oswego, located 34 miles from Syracuse, is the first major port of call offering direct service to all ports in the free world. Photo by Dan Vecchio

Syracuse is one of the largest of New York State's rail markets in carload volume. Photo by Dan Vecchio

Syracuse's "liberation" came on September 24, 1936, when a grand jubilee marked the passing of the last trains through downtown: the westbound Empire State Express and the eastbound Forest City.

Today Conrail maintains a major railyard facility in East Syracuse. As part of a $23 million modernization project completed in 1979, Conrail expanded and computerized the yard. The current system can handle up to 2,200 cars daily, making Syracuse one of the largest of New York State's rail markets in carload volume.

The yard, which is one of the most advanced computer-controlled yards in the country, directs Conrail and Amtrak freight and passenger service to all points in the country. Conrail also offers a special service to bulk commodity shippers. Through the Flexi-Flo service a shipment is loaded at the plant into a covered hopper or tank car that holds about four truckloads. It is then shipped at low-cost, long-haul rail rates to the Flexi-Flo terminal nearest to the ultimate destination. Shipments can then be transferred to trucks for local delivery on an as-needed basis—all in a matter of hours.

AIRWAYS

When "Lucky Lindy" touched down in the *Spirit of St. Louis* at Amboy Field in 1927, all Syracuse celebrated. Charles Lindbergh was hosted and toasted at an offical chamber of commerce dinner, and Syracuse's successful love affair with air travel began.

Until the 1950s Amboy Airport served the air needs of the city. Today Hancock International Airport, just north of downtown Syracuse, is the largest airport in Central New York and the only airport in upstate New York capable of constructing runways that could double airport capacity. Operated by the City of Syracuse, Hancock is conveniently located at the junction of Interstates 81 and 90, making it especially attractive for both freight and passenger service. Over 253 commercial flights depart daily, and almost 3 million passengers pass through Hancock's gates each year. Direct service is provided to over 60 cities in the United States and Canada, and travel connections can be made to any city in the world.

The number one carrier in the Syracuse market is USAir, which serves 50 percent of the passenger traffic. The carrier maintains a major airways hub at the Hancock site. Eight other airlines serving Hancock include American, Continental, Eastern, Northwest, United, Pan Am Express, Mall Airways, and TWA. According to Russell Shedd, Hancock's air-traffic manager, the main runway often handles 45 flight arrivals and departures an hour—one every 80 seconds. Charter aircraft and facilities also are

Handling up to 2,200 cars daily, the Conrail yard in East Syracuse is one of the most advanced computer-controlled yards in the country. Photo by John Dowling

available through Sair Aviation, Jet Management, and Syracuse Executive Air Service.

To accommodate the steady increase in flights and passengers, $5.6 million recently has been invested to expand the North Concourse, and $10 million is budgeted to provide additional gates for the South Concourse. As part of the city's airport expansion project, Hancock recently completed a two-level addition to the South Concourse. It increased the number of gates from 3 to 10, and provided an enlarged office area, a larger customs area, and a presidential suite. The ticket wing was lengthened to provide space for new airlines entering the market, and a second baggage claim area is due to be installed. Ongoing runway improvements include refurbished runway lighting and storm sewer systems, and a stengthened runway surface that will accommodate heavier craft and traffic.

Adding to the growth of Hancock International Airport, the Syracuse Common Council unanimously approved a $10 million plan that will double Hancock's air cargo facility. Hancock International Associates, a local private firm, bought the two existing air cargo hangars from the city for $1.8 million. It is renovating these structures and constructing a new 57,000-square-foot distribution facility at a cost of approximately $8.2 million. The developer will also improve aircraft parking at the site. City of-

ficials and officials of the Greater Syracuse Chamber of Commerce, who worked together to find developers for this project, believe that this facility will eventually compete with New York City area airports. The existing cargo building and parking apron give aircraft direct access to the building and permit quick and efficient cargo handling. Shippers have a variety of options for air freight services. Some of the major air cargo companies with terminals in Syracuse include Airborne Express, Burlington Northern Air Freight, Emery Worldwide, Federal Express, Flying Tigers, Purolator Courier, and United Parcel Service.

Since 2,000 acres of land are available at the Hancock site, city planners are examining proposals for the construction of a second runway parallel to the main runway. If the proposals are carried out, Hancock would become the only airport in upstate New York with parallel runways that could have simultaneous instrument landings.

Air freight services are enhanced by the prime location of Hancock International Airport. Shippers can expect same-day or next-day delivery when shipping to virtually any point in the United States. Shipments to remote points are delivered no later than the second day. Several of the air freight companies serving Syracuse offer international service on a regular basis and will deliver cargo anywhere in the free world.

A revolution in delivery systems has grown from the need of many businesses to find a way to handle a high volume of small package shipments. The need is for speed, efficiency, and inexpensive service. That need has created three basic levels of service: overnight delivery, second-day delivery, and delivery based on the distance involved. Syracuse has over 40 package/courier services offering a variety of methods, costs, and service levels.

Small package shipments to and from the Syracuse area are handled by the United States Postal Service, trucking companies, freight forwarders, airlines, and air freight companies. Companies specializing in small package delivery include Federal Express, Purolator Courier, United Parcel Service, and several local delivery services.

Located in Syracuse is one of the 63 United Parcel Service (UPS) district offices found nationwide. This office controls operations throughout most of upstate New York.

UPS not only has a daily pickup service, but it also maintains a customer counter in East Syracuse. Next-day service is provided to areas such as New York City, Massachusetts, Vermont, and Pennsylvania. Second-day delivery is available to almost anywhere else in the United States and its territories, including Hawaii and Puerto Rico. Service has also been expanded to include delivery to Europe.

Syracuse is one of 86 major area distribution centers (ADCs) in the United States for the U.S. Postal Service. In addition, the Syracuse ADC, located at Taft Road in North Syracuse, processes mail for most of the post offices in Central New York. An average of 2 million pieces of mail pass through the center every day. Syracuse is a successful sectional center because of its close proximity to an airport and major highways. With its Express Mail service, the Postal Service can guarantee next-day delivery to major American cities of packages up to 70 pounds.

Another overnight service is Purolator Courier, which delivers to locations in the entire country via its next-day air express. In addition, in East Syracuse, the rapidly expanding Roadway Package System terminal accepts packages up to 100 pounds and promises second-day delivery for distances up

to 450 miles and fifth-day delivery for 2,100 miles.

Competition for the overnight market is stiff, but many businesses thrive on the activity revolving around these transportation services.

FOREIGN TRADE ZONE

In order to help local industries to compete with foreign markets, the Greater Syracuse Chamber of Commerce advanced legislation to establish a foreign trade zone.

Foreign trade zones are sites where entering and departing goods can be stored and considered by the U.S. Department of Commerce to be out of the customs territory of the United States. Goods can be brought into a zone under customs supervision but without formal entry, the payment of duty, or excise taxes. Only when the goods leave a zone are appropriate charges levied. If the goods are re-exported without ever entering the United States, duty charges and taxes are avoided altogether. Foreign trade zones improve the cash flow position of a business because a company pays duties only on the portion "imported" from the zone, and at the lowest possible final tariff classification. While in the foreign trade zone, goods may be stored, sold, exhibited, repacked, assembled, mixed with foreign and domestic

Many Syracuse businesses thrive on the use of overnight delivery services, such as provided by Emery. Photo by Dan Vecchio

goods, or manufactured into a finished product—all without payment of duties until they are removed from the zone.

The Greater Syracuse Foreign Trade Zone, Ltd., a subsidiary of the chamber, was formed in January 1982. The Paul Jeffery Company, Inc., was selected as the developer and operator of the zone. A sub-zone at Cortland's Smith Corona Corporation was chartered in 1985, entitling that single company to the benefits of the main zone. N. Earle Evans, chairman of the Greater Syracuse Foreign Trade Zone, Ltd., said that the creation of that sub-zone helped Smith Corona battle foreign competition and resulted in a doubling of the company's work force in less than two years.

A second sub-zone was recently approved by the Foreign Trade Zone Division of the U.S. Department of Commerce. This sub-zone is located at Chrysler's New Process Gear plant in the town of DeWitt. Congressman George Wortley, who worked with the chamber on this project, said, "This approval enhances the competitiveness of a key Central New York employer, makes our community a more attractive place in which to do business, offers the promise of economic expansion and, most importantly, creates the

opportunity for additional jobs." Chamber President Erwin Schultz said the sub-zone will stabilize New Process Gear's work force of nearly 3,000 employees, which has an annual payroll of approximately $94 million.

The incentives provided by the existence of the foreign trade zone give Syracuse an advantage in helping businesses to grow and flourish.

PASSENGER TRANSPORTATION

Cars, taxis, buses, trains, and planes—no matter where a person in Syracuse needs to be, there is a way to get there. The city offers a variety of services to commuters and vacationers.

The roadway network provides commuters with both primary and secondary roads that make travel in and out of the city as easy as possible. Camillus, Baldwinsville, Liverpool, North Syracuse, Fayetteville, and Manlius are the suburban areas with the highest concentrations of people commuting to the city. Even at the peak rush hour time between 7:45 a.m. and 8:30 a.m., most of these commuters spend no more than 20 minutes traveling from home to work.

For commuters who prefer public transport, the Central New York Regional Trans-

The sophistication of transportation methods for commercial and public use earned Syracuse 14th place out of 329 metropolitan areas in Rand McNally's Places Rated Almanac. Photo by Dan Vecchio

portation Authority (CENTRO) provides an excellent bus system in the Syracuse area. CENTRO's buses serve the cities of Syracuse in Onondaga County, Fulton and Oswego in Oswego County, and Auburn and surrounding communities in Cayuga County.

Rand McNally's 1985 *Places Rated Almanac* states, "The number of buses available to Syracuse riders, based on total metro population, is well above the national average." CENTRO has a fleet of over 190 full-size vehicles, and it also operates a para-transit service, Call-a-Bus, for the elderly and disabled. Senior citizens and the disabled always ride at half-fare on CENTRO vehicles. In addition to maintaining service

schedules on 19 routes, CENTRO operates employment charters to a number of industrial centers.

CENTRO also recently began operating a system called the Salt City Trolley Route. Quaint-looking vehicles, which run on tires rather than tracks, are all business when it comes to moving commuters, shoppers, and visitors through the streets of downtown Syracuse. The trolley route, coordinated by the City of Syracuse, CENTRO, and the Downtown Committee of Syracuse, is the result of many years of discussion about a parking shuttle system. Now people can park at a designated site near Armory Square and board the Line "B" shuttle for free during

Syracuse offers both commuters and vacationers primary and secondary roads that make travel in and out of the city as easy as possible. Photo by Dan Vecchio

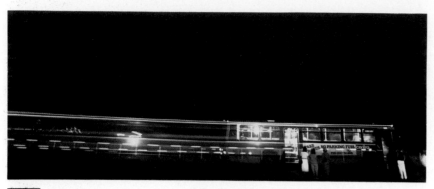

CENTRO, Central New York Regional Transportation Authority, earned the distinction of being named "The Best Mid-Size Transit System in the U.S. and Canada" in 1983 by the American Public Transit Association. Photo by Dan Vecchio

peak commuter hours. This shuttle travels along Onondaga, Warren, Washington, and Franklin streets. A wider area is accommodated by the Line "A" Downtown Loop which, for a dime, takes shoppers and visitors along the scenic route. It travels through Clinton Square, by the Erie Canal Museum and City Hall, through historic Columbus Circle, along "shoppers' row" —where the Galleries of Syracuse, major department stores, and specialty shops are located—and back by the Discovery Center to trendy Armory Square.

CENTRO was distinguished as "The Best Mid-Size Transit System in the U.S. and Canada" in 1983 by the American Public Transit Association. Due to its excellent record for safety, CENTRO also has been acclaimed by the National Safety Council and the American Public Transit Association.

Greyhound and Capital Trailways provide inter-city bus service, and for cities off established routes, numerous charter lines, such as Syracuse and Oswego Motor Lines and Onondaga Coach Corporation, are available. Greyhound, a franchise operation run by a commissioned agent, has daily departures out of Syracuse with substantial increases in departures during peak travel periods.

Amtrak provides passenger rail service. Six departures are made daily from the terminal in East Syracuse, with direct service to New York City and Chicago, and connecting service to other points throughout the United States. Under discussion is a proposal that would provide for a stronger link between rail and bus services. The plan calls for a feeder system of buses departing directly from the Amtrak terminal in East Syracuse for cities such as Watertown, Oswego, Geneva, Seneca Falls, and Auburn. It would enable passengers who need to change modes of transportation to do so more easily.

Hancock International Airport is the center of activity for many commuters and vacationers. More flights depart from Hancock daily than from any other city in New York State except New York City. Many major cities are less than an hour's flight away. Getting to flights or downtown hotels is made easy by Metroplex Taxi and limousine services. In addition, nationally franchised rental services are located within airport facilities, and four other rental agencies situated outside the airport provide shuttle service for their customers. Several local companies provide charter limousine service.

As the day passes, the 35-ton double-wing snowplows return to headquarters in Jamesville and three other zones, standing ready to move out again should a storm hit. For now, they wait.

3:00 p.m.: Out at Hancock Airport, Al Verley heads toward the Executive Air hangar, where he climbs into a Cessna 172 Skyhawk. The ceiling is 1,000 feet above Onondaga Hill, and the visibility is three miles. Snow kept him on the ground with his walkie-talkie this morning. This afternoon he can do what he loves best: report traffic from the air.

3:30 p.m.: Al broadcasts his first "ride-home" report for WSYR's Skyview Traffic. "Traffic is moving along at Sweetheart Corners. Two turns of the light should get you through," he tells motorists. Downtown is next. Below there is a disabled vehicle by the Harrison-Adams ramp. Between reports he tells the station to alert the police. He guides drivers into other lanes, and the traffic flows on.

While he keeps an eye on the ground below, Al keeps his ears tuned to 14 bands on his scanner. Every 10 minutes he broadcasts tie-ups, slowdowns, and ways to avoid delays.

5:50 p.m.: With the last report called in, Al banks toward Hancock. He likes what he does because he knows that he provides a good service to commuters. "And the sunrises and sunsets—they make it all worthwhile," he says.

Downtown buildings absorb the magenta skyscape, and window lights wink on.

Another day has almost ended. Syracuse is safely home.

Above: Another working day has ended for these commuters headed home. Photo by Dan Vecchio

This advanced-technology Conrail yard is able to direct Conrail and Amtrak freight and passenger service to all points in the country. Photo by John Dowling

Though simple in appearance, these wires represent an economical and efficient communication network in the Syracuse area. Photo by John Dowling

Chapter Three

Powering the Community
Utilities and Communication Networks

by Alexis O'Neill

T hat couch-side reading light. That cool summertime room. That call from Mom. That refreshing glass of water. That favorite song. That special story. Each is ours with little more effort than reaching for a switch, phone, faucet, or paper. These are conveniences that we often take for granted, yet they are part of important, basic networks that power our community and bring resources and information conveniently to our doorsteps. In the Greater Syracuse region, these networks are more than pipes, wires, cables, and airwave transmissions. These networks are also composed of people committed both to providing what consumers have come to expect and to developing and providing other related services to the community.

DIVERSE ENERGY BASE

From the four oil lamps installed to light the village of Syracuse in 1825, to the gas lamps which were not lighted on evenings when moon was full, to the first electrical arc lamp beaming down from the Weiting Opera House in 1878, Greater Syracuse's energy system grew in size and technological sophistication. Nearly 200 separate companies were formed in the central region, and scores of other electric and gas entities existed in the early days of power production and distribution. By 1937, however, only 12 operating companies remained. At that point they were consolidated to create a single company, Central New York Power Corporation. This firm, in turn, was one of the three major companies which in 1950 formed

Niagara Mohawk Power Corporation (NiMo), the largest supplier of electricity and gas in upstate New York. The consolidation made it possible to run operations economically and efficiently, integrate facilities, and standardize procedures.

Niagara Mohawk Power Corporation, a $2.6 billion utility, provides electricity and natural gas to more than 3.6 million people in 37 upstate New York counties. NiMo's commitment is not only to providing diversified, economical resources for power, but to conserving energy so that the resources are not depleted.

In New York State, electric power is supplied by seven investor-owned utilities and the Power Authority of the State of New York (PASNY), a public benefit corporation engaged in bulk power generation. As members of the New York State Power Pool, Niagara Mohawk and other utilities coordinate electrical production and transmission statewide, including the provision of electrical power in the event of emergencies. The result of the inter-utility cooperation is reasonably priced electricity regardless of demand. This assures both residences and businesses of a continuous, reliable flow of affordable electricity.

NiMo's electricity comes from a mix of generating sources, including nuclear, coal, gas, and hydro power. Because of this, the rates are the lowest of any set by investor-owned utilities in a tri-state area. In a comparison of major electric power companies in this area (New York, New Jersey, and Connecticut), NiMo's typical monthly electric bill for an average family in a recent summer was $38.27 compared with the next lowest in New York State, $48.96 in Rochester, and lows of $47.74 in New Jersey and $48.27 in Connecticut. Greater Syracuse businesses are paying up to 30 percent less for electricity than the state and Mid-Atlantic averages. Residential users' bills are below the state, regional, and national averages.

Much of the natural wealth of the Greater Syracuse area lies in its abundant water resources. From small waterfalls in the Adirondacks to the thundering magnificence of Niagara Falls, many sources are tapped for hydroelectric generation, which accounts for 30 percent of the supply of energy. In the total power mix, 18 percent is derived from coal, 14 percent from nuclear energy, 11 percent from oil, 4 percent from natural gas, and the remaining 23 percent from various purchased power sources.

Hydroelectric power is the most economical source of energy. Over the past few years Niagara Mohawk has initiated an ambitious hydro-expansion program. Currently NiMo operates 77 hydro generating plants, more than are operated by any other utility in the free world. The largest of these plants are the Rankin Station on the Niagara River at Niagara Falls and the Spirer Station on the Hudson River. In addition, Hydra-Co Enterprises, Inc., a subsidiary of Niagara Mohawk, has been formed to market and construct co-generation, steam-electric energy plants and small hydroelectric projects.

Five fossil-fuel generating stations provide the power system's backbone, guaranteeing reliable energy service in spite of variances in demand. These stations, situated in Buffalo, Dunkirk, Albany, Oswego, and Newburgh, are fired with coal, oil, and natural gas. NiMo pays a lower price per BTU of coal than any utility in the state and has lowered oil costs by about 35 percent since 1981.

Niagara Mohawk is a retailer of natural gas, purchasing its full supply from the Consolidated Gas Supply Corporation. This company serves 433,000 gas customers throughout New York State, with supply lines extending from Pennsylvania through the southern tier of New York and northward into Onondaga County to Skaneateles, Otisco, and Tully. There the connection is made with NiMo's 6,495-mile system of pipelines and mains, which takes the gas to its customers.

In April 1979 the Public Service Commission authorized Niagara Mohawk to bill its customers in terms of heat content rather than volume. Therefore, gas customers are now billed in therms rather than cubic feet of gas. In 1984 the amount of gas available to serve a new industrial customer was unlimited.

Local involvement with nuclear power began in the 1950s. At that time NiMo joined the Atomic Power Development Associates with the encouragement of the federal government. Staff engineers were assigned to the Enrico Fermi atomic power project in Michigan, and in late 1969 Nine Mile Point Nuclear Station Unit Number One went into commercial operation. Nine

Mile One, as it is called, is located on Lake Ontario near Oswego.

Nuclear Engineering International, a British trade magazine, recently called the Nine Mile One nuclear plant near Oswego the most productive boiling-water reactor in the United States and the seventh most productive in the world. The publication cited Nine Mile One after surveying and ranking 325 nuclear plants operating in the western world for its "Nuclear Station Achievement List for 1987." Plants were ranked by their capacity factor—the amount of energy produced compared with the rated generating capacity over a specified period of time.

The 610-megawatt Nine Mile One, owned and operated by NiMo, has been in service longer than any of the other 10 top-rated U.S. reactors in the 1987 survey. In October 1987 Nine Mile One set a national record for 415 days of uninterrupted operation, falling just 42 hours short of a world record. During this record run it operated at 94.6 percent of capacity. More than 60 billion kilowatt hours of electricity have been generated in the plant's 18 years of operation—the equivalent of approximately 102 million barrels of oil.

The completion of Nine Mile Two has added a plant with a 1,084-megawatt capacity to the electrical network. Nine Mile Two is jointly owned by Niagara Mohawk (41 percent), Long Island Lighting Company (18 percent), New York State Electric and Gas Corporation (18 percent), Rochester Gas and Electric Corporation (14 percent), and Central Hudson Gas and Electric Corporation (9 percent). Nine Mile Two was able to supply more than 335 million kilowatt-hours of power to the New York power grid in the 1987 testing period.

In addition, Niagara Mohawk is involved in a number of research projects involving solar, thermal storage, heat pump, and fuel cell programs which focus on the development and conservation of energy sources. In 1986 NITECH was established to produce and market the Power-Donut Sensor Line Monitoring System. This system measures vital conditions affecting load carrying capability. NiMo's heat pump project, begun in 1982, won both the New York Governor's Award for Energy Innovation and national recognition from the U.S. Department of Energy.

In the Greater Syracuse area, NiMo

Nine Mile Two adds a 1,084 megawatt capacity to the 610 megawatt Nine Mile One electrical network. Photo by Mike Okoniewski

offers existing businesses and new industries favorable energy rates as well as advice on cost-saving systems and techniques for improving energy efficiency. Since 1984 it also has offered discounted prices to approximately 90 businesses that have expanded within this area. Other discounts are being offered to businesses planning to expand or relocate in state-approved economic development zones, and to financially troubled companies with viable revitalization strategies.

NiMo provides many additional services to customers. Time-of-use pricing, which has been available to industrial and commercial users that take advantage of energy during off-peak periods, is now being tested with residential users. Through the free Saving Power Survey Program, customers can receive an energy conservation survey and receive low- and no-cost loans to make recommended improvements. In order to help elderly, disabled, and chronically ill consumers to cover energy-related emergencies, NiMo began the Care & Share Energy Fund in 1984. Employees, shareholders, and customers donated more than one million dollars to this fund, which is administered by the American Red Cross.

WATER

Skaneateles Lake. Otisco Lake. Salmon River. Seneca River. Oneida Lake. Oneida River. Butternut Creek. Lake Ontario. Some call the supply of clean water in the Greater Syracuse area limitless.

In 1889, the same year that the Greater Syracuse Chamber of Commerce began, an overwhelming majority of the local voters approved a $3 million bond issue to bring

Bristol Laboratories is among the several non-contact cooling and water processing plants used in the Syracuse area. Photo by Joe Martin

water 19 miles from Skaneateles Lake to Syracuse. As one of the Finger Lakes, Skaneateles Lake provided 14 square miles of surface, a watershed of 73 square miles, and clear, cool depths ranging down to 300 feet. While the residents of Skaneateles were not anxious to share this bountiful resource with the Syracuse "city folk," the work began anyway. When the long-awaited day arrived in 1894, Skaneateles Lake water was turned on at the Woodland Reservoir gate house. Four days later, on July 3, it arrived in Syracuse. Celebrants grabbed handles from a wagon loaded with tin dippers, and 100 guns saluted the landmark event. The city's population soon rose from 87,000 to 215,000, with another 206,000 in the suburbs.

Skaneateles Lake is still the primary water source for the city of Syracuse, and it has received an AAA special water quality classification. It produces almost 50 million gallons of water per day.

As productive as the existing system was, local citizens and community leaders in the twentieth century knew that this supply could not provide all the water needed for residential, commercial, and industrial expansion. In one of the most significant local engineering developments of the century, a 25-mile pipeline was built that connected Onondaga County with Lake Ontario and its unlimited supply of good water. One of the Great Lakes, Lake Ontario covers over 8,000 square miles and is fed by a 40,000-square-mile watershed that receives an average of 24

inches of rainfall a year.

Engineered by a local firm, O'Brien & Gere, the Lake Ontario Project was approved in separate votes by both city and county residents in 1965. It was financed by a $45 million bond issue, and it engaged the cooperation of the Metropolitan Water Board and the Onondaga County Water Authority. The project involved the construction of both the pipeline and distribution system needed to bring water from the Great Lakes to Onondaga County. Although the vote was not an easy one to win, and "The Battle of Lake Ontario" began in earnest in 1962, by 1967, 36 million gallons of water were being pumped into Onondaga County each day.

Today, interconnecting pipelines, each with its own source, assure Greater Syracuse of a constant supply of water even when high demands are placed on the system. The sources include Lake Ontario to the north and two of the Finger Lakes, Otisco and Skaneateles, to the southwest.

An assured, high quality water supply is especially important to local corporations such as Anheuser-Busch, Bristol Laboratories, Miller Brewing Company, and Syracuse China, which are all non-contact cooling and process water users. The region's supply of clean water helps ensure their future success.

The Lake Ontario pipeline was designed with an eye toward the future. When the initial 54-inch pipe and pumping stations were first built, a system of parallel conduits was also installed in tunnels and rivers, allowing a second pipeline to be built easily and economically should the need arise. In addition, the pipeline right-of-way is large enough to allow even greater expansion. This guarantees the Greater Syracuse area not only the source but the system to handle this natural resource for years to come.

Syracusans currently use just over 76 percent of the system's capacity of 131 million gallons a day. Should demand increase, an output of 300 million gallons a day is possible. New York State boasts the highest water quality standards in the nation, and Syracuse exceeds them.

Compared to rates in other regions of the country, the cost of water in the Syracuse area is low. Rates within the Greater Syracuse area vary depending upon the distribution system, the location, and the amount used. As an example, however, an industry using one million gallons a day has been known to pay as little as 59 cents and no more than 72 cents for 1,000 gallons.

Greater Syracuse also has a comprehensive system for wastewater treatment. When water has been used in homes and industries, it goes through a network of pipes to one of the 10 sewage treatment plants operated by the Onondaga County Department of Drainage and Sanitation. When water cannot reach the plants by gravity alone, 90 pumping stations move the water to treatment. The technologically advanced plants provide local consumers with better quality treated water than is typically found across the country.

The Consolidated Sanitary District extends throughout Onondaga County, serving not only the city but the outlying areas of this metropolitan region as well. Current usage is approximately 73 percent of capacity, so there is room for additional use by new industries and residences. In the past few years smaller plants have been eliminated and replaced by larger, more efficient facilities, changing the total number of plants from 12 to 10. There are also five independent plants in Onondaga County in the villages of Jordan, Marcellus, Minoa, Tully, and Skaneateles.

A prime responsibility is monitoring the amount of waste disposed of daily and examining used water to determine the exact levels of contaminants in the water. Since 1973 the Onondaga County Department of Drainage and Sanitation has been conducting a successful industrial waste monitoring program.

TELEPHONE SERVICE

In a time when telephones are found in almost every room in the house as well as in cars, it is hard to imagine a time when Syracusans took little interest in Alexander Graham Bell's wondrous invention. Yet from 1876 to 1878 the only conversations over the phone wire in Syracuse took place between Fred Brower and his father, who owned a local hardware store. This modest spark of interest was fanned in 1878 by a much-heralded demonstration at the Weiting Theater of instrumental and vocal music phoned from Auburn. By 1887 more than 250 people subscribed to the local exchange.

Today no local subscriber needs to be convinced of the many benefits of the phone system: more than 102 million calls are made throughout the state each business day. Among the many services offered to customers are touchtone dialing, three-way calling, call waiting, speed dialing, call forwarding, and international direct dialing.

It was not unusual for an installer of the 1880s to carry over 100 pounds of equipment when out on a job, including a 50-pound telephone. It also was not unusual for an operator to work nine hours a day, six days a week. The service itself inspired great loyalty among those who worked for what was originally called the Central New York Telephone and Telegraph Company. Syracuse newspaper accounts tell of operators braving tremendous storms in order to attend to the switchboards.

While employees still have a great commitment to serving the public quickly and efficiently, the days of the one-stop telephone company ended with deregulation in 1984. The advantage was the creation of a competitive marketplace for telecommunications equipment and services in the Greater Syracuse region. Currently there are over 20 vendors of telecommunications products as well as of data processing and long distance services.

With the breakup of the Bell System in January 1984, New York Telephone was no longer a subsidiary of American Telephone and Telegraph. It became a wholly owned subsidiary of the NYNEX Corporation, which is also the parent company of New England Telephone and Telegraph. New York Telephone currently employs about 3,240 people in Central New York, about 1,600 of whom work in the Syracuse metropolitan area. It provides a switching system and intelligence network, and it continues to be the area's primary supplier of telephone lines and related central office equipment.

Through New York Telephone, customers receive basic exchange service along with long distance service within geographic areas known as Local Access and Transport Areas (LATAs). The Central New York LATA includes the 315 area code and the Ithaca/Cortland portion of the 607 area. Other long distance carriers such as AT&T, MCI, and U.S. Sprint handle any calls outside the LATA boundaries.

With a 1984 construction budget of about $7 million in the city of Syracuse and

New York Telephone is the area's primary supplier of telephone lines and related central office features. Photo by John Dowling

York Telephone and NYNEX are major corporate contributors to the Syracuse University Center for Science and Technology. In addition, New York Telephone is working with Syracuse University to outfit each student's dormitory room so the student can have both on-line access to the university's mainframe computer and use of the room's telephone.

Deregulation stimulated healthy competition in Greater Syracuse, as it did in many parts of the country. It created an active marketplace for telecommunications equipment and services. Current leaders in equipment supplies include NYNEX Business Information Systems and Tel Plus Communications, which offers hardware and services to consumers. Several companies have specialized in mobile communications, including Cellular One and NYNEX Mobile Communications. They equip customers' car phones with a full range of services such as call waiting, call forwarding, no-answer transfer, and call conferencing.

POSTAL SERVICE

If it had not been for the area's first postmaster in 1820, citizens might still be arguing over a name for Syracuse, and this book might have had a significantly different title. Salt manufacturers favored "Salina," Erie Canal proponents favored "Clinton," and many others favored "Corinth." That is, until Postmaster John Wilkinson, a prominent citizen, discovered another town bearing the name of Corinth. In his search for a replacement, Wilkinson remembered reading about a city called Siracusa on a lake in Sicily, which had salt deposits and a neighboring town called Salina. The uncanny similarities led him to suggest the name "Syracuse." As one broadcaster says, you know the rest of the story.

Since Wilkinson, Syracuse has had 25 U.S. postmasters managing communications for consumers who now total 1.24 million locally. The U.S. Postal Service Management Sectional Center (MSC) at Syracuse operates 203 post offices and 29 stations and branches in its 7,860-square-mile service area. More than 3,000 people are employed to ensure efficient, dependable delivery of mail and associated services to 245,000 city and rural delivery points each day.

Located on East Taft Road, the Syracuse MSC is one of 86 distribution centers in the

some $48 million in Central New York, New York Telephone upgraded and expanded its network services, a program that still continues. Several million dollars have been invested to convert the entire city of Syracuse and most of the suburbs to all electronic switching. This service provides customers with more reliable service, high-speed data transmissions, clarity, custom calling options, and lower maintenance costs.

New York Telephone uses state-of-the-art technology for high-speed data communications and, through the use of fiber optics, is capable of meeting higher volume demands in the future. To further enhance the quality of life in the Syracuse area, New

United States. It processes mail for most of the post offices in Central New York and for incoming mail from around the world going to Binghamton and Utica. The Syracuse General Mail Facility occupies 53.5 acres, with 6.9 acres under roof. During the 1987 fiscal year alone, the Syracuse MSC handled 720.5 million pieces of mail—an average of 2.3 million pieces daily—with 98 percent reaching destinations overnight. State-of-the-art mail processing equipment ensures the speedy delivery rate. The equipment includes bar code sorters, optical character readers, and multiposition letter sorting machines. Up to 38,000 pieces of mail are sorted per hour.

Stations and branches are at convenient locations throughout the Greater Syracuse area. The Taft Road facility is only one mile from Syracuse's Hancock International Airport. Services for customers range from the familiar window sales of stamps to bulk mail acceptance to providing account representatives who work closely with major customers.

PRINT AND ELECTRONIC MEDIA

The Greater Syracuse region is never at a loss for words. Or music for that matter. With over 26 newspapers, 15 radio stations, and 7 television stations—as well as scores of publications produced by local industries, institutions, and businesses, and 49 other Central New York newspapers—residents do not have to look far to keep up with news, information, and pure entertainment.

Heavyweights among the print media include two major dailies, the morning *Post-Standard* and the evening *Herald-Journal*, with the *Herald* having the greatest share of the market. Both newspapers have roots reaching back to the early nineteenth century.

The *Journal* began in 1839 and became a daily in 1844. When hard times descended at the turn of the century, it was purchased by Harvey Burrill, the son of a salt manufacturer. Arthur Jenkins published the first edition of the rival *Herald* on January 15, 1877. When William Randolph Hearst came to town in 1925, he consolidated the *Syracuse Telegram,* the *Syracuse Sunday American,* and the *Syracuse Journal,* to the displeasure of the community. In 1939 the Hearst era ended when Samuel I. Newhouse purchased the *Herald* and the *Syracuse Journal* and merged them.

68 WSYT is one of the leading television stations in the city. Photo by Reflections Unlimited

The turn of the century also saw the growth of the *Post-Standard,* which survived the rash of newspapers that proliferated during the canal and Civil War eras. A politically oriented paper, the *Standard* was known for its role in social issues such as the abolitionist movement. When it became a daily in 1850, it was designated the official city paper. In 1899, however, when it became the *Post-Standard,* the paper's editorial staff prided itself on not having won the blessings of the mayor.

Syracuse's "alternative" newspaper is *The Syracuse New Times,* a free weekly that has a circulation of over 53,000. Articles in the *New Times* address controversial issues, and its calendar provides one of the area's most comprehensive listings of arts and entertainment opportunities.

A variety of prestigious weekly papers serve the suburbs. The oldest is the *Skaneateles Press,* which was founded in 1829. Other well-established suburban papers include the Fayetteville-Manlius area's *Eagle Bulletin/Suburban Life,* which dates back to 1877, and the *Cazenovia Republican.* Communities to the north are served by the *Baldwinsville Messenger,* the *Liverpool-Salina Review,* the *Syracuse Star News,* and the *Town Crier.* The *Onondaga Valley News* serves the southern region, while *The Advocate* in Camillus serves the west. Specialized papers include *The Catholic Sun, Jewish Observer, The Impartial Citizen,* and *The Syracuse Banner News.*

Radio stations also abound in the Greater Syracuse area. The battle of the airwaves is waged daily as local broadcasters seek greater listening audiences. This invigorating competition has served the local

WTVH-5, originally WHEN-TV, was a pioneer in television broadcasting in 1948, producing ground-breaking shows such as *The Magic Toyshop* for children. Its award-winning tradition continues today. Photo by John Dowling

consumer well, particularly as stations tailor programming to reach more specific markets—a strategy which not only provides listeners with entertainment, but also helps advertisers reach intended audiences more easily.

Currently there are 19 radio stations in the Syracuse area: 5 are FM only, and 7 provide both AM and FM programs. Shows appeal to a wide variety of listening tastes: jazz, rock, public service, easy listening, country, adult contemporary, Christian, great gold, news, and nostalgia.

Primary competitors in the AM market are Radio 57/WSYR and 62 WHEN. The top-rated station at present is Radio 57/WSYR, which provides both adult contemporary music and complete information services. Y94 FM, its sister station, has a morning show with Big Mike live. Big Mike was again nominated by *Billboard* magazine in 1988 as Radio Personality of the Year. He has won this national award three times in the past. Sports fans tune in to the "Voice of the Orange" for Syracuse University sports, news fans hear a 90-minute comprehensive broadcast during their ride home from work, and advice fans can flip the volume up on "Talknet" seven nights a week.

62 WHEN has earned a reputation for both its entertaining programming and its deep commitment to the daily life of the community. This commitment is demonstrated through its "Call for Action" consumer advocacy line, "Media Weather," and Captain Scott King's air traffic report. Over the years, services provided by 62 WHEN to Central New Yorkers have earned the station recognition from the National Weather Service, the Department of Transportation, and the U.S. Congress.

For public broadcasting, Central New Yorkers can tune in to WCNY-FM, or WRVO-FM, or WAER, which offer public service, classical music, and jazz programs.

In television's infant days, there were only three places outside of New York City that boasted their own stations. Syracuse became one of those three television pioneers when WHEN-TV (now WTVH-5) made its first broadcast in 1948.

Picture this: a city with only 40 television sets, most in taverns or department store showrooms. Crowds peer over shoulders at the small round screens. Suddenly, the image of a man and a harp appears, and Syracusans take a major step into the age of electronic media. As local store owner Melville Clark played the harp on screen, did anyone dream of the day when satellites would beam from all parts of the earth, making the world smaller and smaller with each transmission?

WTVH-5, a CBS affiliate, was a groundbreaker in many ways. It introduced remote coverage and produced the longest-running children's program in history, "The Magic Toy Shop." The station's involvement with the community has been reflected in the careful production of its award-winning documentary, "Something Special," and other public affairs programming.

Other network stations are WSTM-TV (an NBC affiliate on Channel 3) and WIXT-TV (an ABC affiliate on Channel 9). Each station has distinctive services that it provides to the Greater Syracuse community. WSTM-TV sponsors "For Kids' Sake" programs, events, and messages which increase awareness of the problems and challenges facing young people today. A prime-time show, "The Gift of Time," highlighted the contributions of adults who have spent countless hours in service to youngsters. At a local mall WSTM-TV sponsored a "Kids Against Drugs Day" featuring former Syracuse University football star Joe Morris and supported by many other community groups, including the local chapter of Students Against Drunk Driving. Messages on television, which are aimed at both parents and children, include advice on topics such as nutrition, safety, and quality time. Calling itself "The News Station," WSTM-TV also provides comprehensive coverage throughout its daily schedule, including the "Today Show" in the morning, noontime news, and news at 6 and 11 p.m.

WIXT-TV's commitment is to "make good things happen for Central New York" by providing interesting broadcasts for viewing audiences as well as needed services to the community. As a result WIXT has made a name for itself in the area of health issues. Newscaster Carrie Lazarus produces the popular "Health Cast" five nights a week, and WIXT sponsors many health-related events such as the Heart Run, the Syracuse University Health Fair, the Miracle Network Telethon, and events for the Cancer Society.

The Greater Syracuse region also enjoys alternative, non-commercial broadcasting through one public television station, one independent television station, and two cable systems.

WCNY-TV, Central New York's public television station, has a membership of 23,000 and over 500,000 viewers per week in its service area. The broadcast area covers 10 counties, with residents of Onondaga, Oswego, and Madison counties comprising more than 400,000 members of the total viewing audience. National programs combine with locally originated programs to provide commercial-free viewing. Shows focusing on children, business, the fine arts, the performing arts, public affairs, science, and nature are all part of the weekly schedule.

Many of WCNY's locally produced programs have been purchased by national markets. They include a 13-part jazz series; a show called "Now Tell Us About the War," featuring reminiscences of Vietnam veterans; "Old Enough to Care," a 6-part series on aging; and a series on bluegrass music. Each year in June, WCNY holds its largest fund-raising event, "TelAuc," one of the 10 largest televised auctions of its kind in the country. In 1987 "TelAuc" raised a half-million dollars for WCNY.

The local independent television station is WSYT-Channel 68, one of the region's newest broadcasting choices. Nostalgia and prime-time programming are featured by this Fox network affiliate. WSYT also provides exclusive television coverage of SU basketball games.

Cooke CableVision and NewChannels provide a wide variety of cable-related services to the community. In addition to regular programming for 36,500 subscribers in the city of Syracuse, Cooke CableVision provides an access channel on which community organizations can present their own programs. The Cooke staff provides training in script preparation, equipment use, and final product editing. The most successful of these programs has been the award-winning "Rough Times Live," an issues-oriented program designed by and for teenagers. NewChannels, which has its corporate offices in Greater Syracuse, serves 34 suburban areas and has a subscribership of 66,000. Established in 1974, NewChannels now has a 41-channel line-up, the most expansive in Central New York.

Greater Syracuse's exemplary reputation in the field of communications is further enhanced by Syracuse University's S.I. Newhouse School of Public Communications.

Communications as an academic discipline began at Syracuse University in 1937, and it was housed at one time in Yates Castle on Irving Avenue. The school has since become the Newhouse Communications Center, and it is among the world's most advanced centers for the study of mass communications. Newhouse I, a building designed by renowned architect I.M. Pei, is primarily devoted to print and photography, while Newhouse II is devoted to television, radio, and film. More than 2,000 of SU's 11,000 undergraduates are enrolled as majors in advertising, broadcast journalism, magazines, newspapers, photography, public relations, or television, radio, and film. Faculty members comprise a distinguished group of specialists and practitioners who advocate an appropriate blend of theory and real-life experience. Students take an active part in projects throughout the Greater Syracuse region as well as in such major cities as New York, Los Angeles, and London.

In Greater Syracuse today, unseen networks of pipes, wires, and cables run beneath the feet of residents, and airwaves enhanced by media programming surround their heads. They enjoy the products that technology brings within their reach—illumination, warmth, sustenance, and culture. The utilities and communications networks that power the area are among the best in the country. They not only provide efficient, economical, and enlightened basic services, but they make a point of providing extra services that contribute to the high quality of living in the Greater Syracuse region.

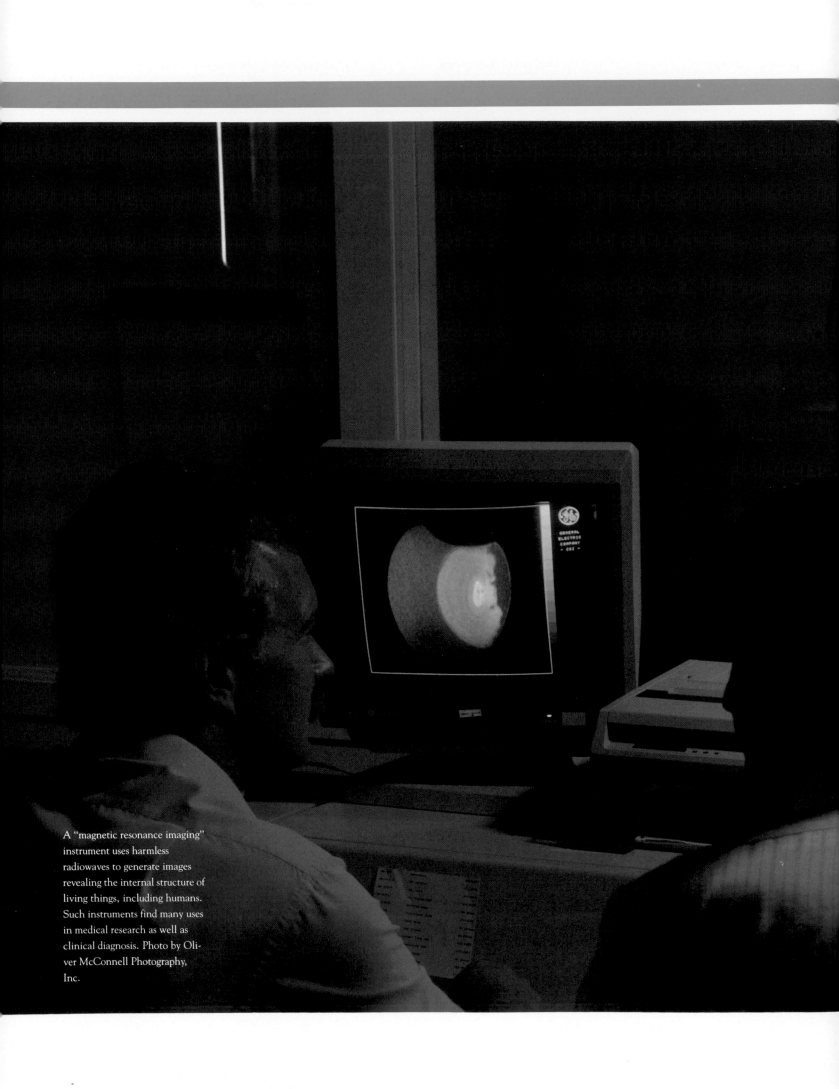

A "magnetic resonance imaging" instrument uses harmless radiowaves to generate images revealing the internal structure of living things, including humans. Such instruments find many uses in medical research as well as clinical diagnosis. Photo by Oliver McConnell Photography, Inc.

Chapter Four

Creating Jobs in the Community
Manufacturing

by Joseph A. Porcello

Reports about the demise of manufacturing in the Syracuse area, like the rumors of Mark Twain's death, are "grossly exaggerated," in the words of the noted author who wrote his immortal tales of Tom Sawyer and Huckleberry Finn in Elmira only 85 miles south of Syracuse.

Manufacturing is not only alive, it is thriving in the Syracuse area. The number of Syracuse area industrial companies has been growing—and still is. Industrial payrolls also have increased substantially, despite problems that have resulted in lower employment at manufacturing plants. Welcome trends are the plans of some local manufacturers to remain and expand in the area and the openings of new companies.

Total employment in the Syracuse area showed a one percent increase through the third quarter of 1987—a gain of 3,000 new jobs—despite the heavy manufacturing job loss in 1986 and 1987, reported Erwin G. Schultz, president of the Greater Syracuse Chamber of Commerce, in January 1988.

"The year ended on an upward trend and with enough momentum to allow us to project 5,000 new jobs in 1988," Schultz said. He said that many of those jobs will come from tremendous growth in small manufacturing. He also noted that "the hard data, those figures that tell us where we're at and where we're going, were generally positive last year."

Rising employment cut the unemployment rate to 4.2 percent in June–July 1988, a record low for the Syracuse metropolitan

Crisp lines denote the James M. Hanley Federal Building on Clinton Street. Photo by Robert H. Schulz, Jr.

firms, increasing the area's high technology industry segment and helping metropolitan Syracuse to recover from industrial job losses. Among new companies locating in the Syracuse area with the assistance of the Greater Syracuse Chamber of Commerce are Electronic Ballast Technology (fluorescent lighting equipment), Certelecom Laboratories (telecommunications testing), and Eastman Kodak's Fastek unit (special filters).

Ten of the 21 tenants in the Greater Syracuse Business Center (the chamber's business incubator) in early 1988 were in high-tech fields, including computer-related firms, one bonding ceramics to copper for semiconductors, and another providing special molded plastics for industry.

The latest directory of industrial firms issued by the Greater Syracuse Chamber of Commerce and the Manufacturers Association of Central New York includes such new members as CID Technologies Inc. (electronic video cameras), Cable Express (cables and cabling for IBM mainframe computers), Reynoldstech Fabricators Inc. (process systems for the semiconductor industry), as well as Certelecom and Fastek.

These newcomers join the many high technology companies that make the Syracuse area a magnet for firms in related technological industries.

The General Electric Company, with its Electronic Laboratory and its Radar Systems and Undersea Systems (GE's military defense electronics design, development, and manufacturing departments), is both the area's largest high-tech company and its biggest industrial employer. GE's Radar Systems Department and Undersea Systems Department, which produces sonar systems, have made GE a leader among defense contractors. The two military defense equipment departments employ 90 percent of GE's 6,000 workers in the Syracuse area. The Electronic Laboratory and Projection Display Products Operation, which produces large screen projection systems, are the other two local GE units.

The Undersea Systems Department (USD) in December 1987 won a major U.S. Navy contract which will total about $1.5 billion over several years, the largest ever received by USD. The contract, which is expected to increase USD's professional staffs by about 400 people over the next few years, is for full-scale development and

Central New York," Schneider commented.

Most of the new investment is in the newest available technology, production equipment, and machinery, which helps manufacturers to improve quality, employee productivity, and competitiveness while helping to reduce costs and holding down price increases.

Also, many of the new companies coming to Central New York are technolgy-based

limited production of a combat control-acoustic system for U.S. attack submarines, including integration and control of all on-board weapons systems. Work began on the contract in 1988 and is slated for completion in 1995. Any additional growth in GE's local departments will depend on the company's ability to win additional defense contracts from the United States and its allies, according to the company. GE shipped radar systems to South Korea, Egypt, and Saudi Arabia in 1987. The E-Lab continues to provide high technology expertise to important company programs at a number of GE locations through its research on integrated circuits, electro-optics, transistors, and sensors.

Additional impetus for high-tech industries is expected to come from Syracuse University and its sophisticated research programs, including the new Center for Computer Applications and Software Engineering (CASE Center), one of seven Centers for Advanced Technology created by the state. CASE Center research focuses on increasing the productivity and reliability of computer software and on other computer-related areas. Another SU high-tech unit, the Northeast Parallel Architecture Center, conducts basic research in parallel computing, which uses several computers to process various portions of a major project simultaneously (in parallel) for a quicker solution. Both SU centers are expected to spin off high technology manufacturing and commercial firms, as has happened in the past.

Other Syracuse area high technology leaders include Carrier Corporation, New York Telephone Company, Niagara Mohawk Power Corporation, Microwave Filter Company, Anaren Microwave Inc., GTE, B.G. Sulzle Inc., Microwave/Systems Inc., Genigraphics Corporation, and many other companies.

In addition, 88 of the MACNY survey respondents, representing the employers of 88.1 percent of Onondaga County's manufacturing work force, indicated that their industries' economic outlook for the first six months of 1988 was either improved over the previous half year or stable. A stable or improved industrial outlook was expected nationally by 78 percent of the companies.

The survey findings support Schultz's statement that increases in employment will come principally in small to medium-sized companies—those with 250 employees or less. That would include over 90 percent of MACNY's members. Only 28 of the organization's nearly 450 members employ 200 or more people. Some 70 percent of the manufacturers belonging to MACNY employ less than 50 workers.

The survey findings provide additional confirmation for the results of numerous previous studies which have shown that small and medium-sized firms create the great majority of new jobs—with estimates ranging up to 90 percent of the annual total. Other studies have found that nearly all of a community's job growth will come from its small and medium-sized firms, generally among companies that are already in the area or start there.

Small companies create thousands of jobs annually—if for no other reason, because there are so many of them in comparison with large companies. Simply stated, if 1,000 small companies add one employee each year as they grow, 1,000 new jobs are created.

All of the 15 manufacturing companies which joined MACNY in 1987 employed fewer than 200 people. Thirteen had fewer than 50 employees, and 5 had fewer than 10 workers. All but two of these manufacturers had been started in the area, and six of them had opened within the previous three years.

PICO Products, Inc., and its subsidiaries design, manufacture, import, and market a wide range of products which receive, distribute, and secure telecommunication signals. Photo by David Revette Photography

Heid's hot dog stand in Liverpool, in business since 1886, is a Syracuse landmark. Photo by Robert Schulz, Jr.

Chapter Five

Supplying the Goods
Retail and Wholesale

by Joseph A. Porcello

The Syracuse area, because of its geographical advantages, was a natural trading area even before the Erie Canal and the arrival of the railroad. The city's first "emporium" grew out of a store started by Thomas McCarthy in the early nineteenth century. After the Civil War, almost 100 years after the coming of the first permanent white settlers, the early versions of today's modern department, specialty, and variety stores first appeared in Syracuse.

The original McCarthy Store has been closed for nearly a century, but some other early retailers—such locally owned businesses as Dey Brothers and C.E. Chappell, and national chains like Sears Roebuck & Co., K mart, and JCPenney—still play major roles in the Syracuse retailing market. During the last 30 years, more and more new department stores and specialty chains have opened in Central New York.

But quite a lot has changed. Since the 1960s, in Syracuse and around the nation, a new dimension has been added to retailing. The development of covered shopping malls and the expansion and conversion of existing shopping centers into roofed-over store and service complexes has changed the way the retail trade is conducted. Modern food supermarkets also are vastly different than the general stores where Syracuse residents of the early nineteenth century bartered for staples like flour and sugar, cloth, kitchen utensils, tools, and other needed small items.

The giant "superstores" of regional food

Marine Midland is a major financial institution in the city. Photo by Jerry Fine

first mayor, and other businessmen formed the Syracuse Savings Bank. Until 1987 Syracuse Savings was the area bank that had operated as the same company and under the same name for the longest time. That year Syracuse Savings was acquired by Norstar Bank, and the name on all branches, including its downtown landmark sandstone headquarters, was changed to Norstar.

In 1855 Onondaga County Savings Bank, which was not related to the Onondaga County Bank of 1830, opened its doors for business and started the operations that

have taken it to over a billion dollars in assets.

EARLY MEDICINE, LAW, AND INSURANCE

The beginnings of medical, legal, and other services started long before the first bank. Some physicians and lawyers were helping patients and clients in the 1790s.

Dr. William Needham is believed to be the first physician to open offices in Syracuse, which he did in 1793. Additional doctors followed soon after to tend to the growing number of area residents. By 1806 the area had some 20 doctors. That year the Onondaga Medical Society was organized by local doctors to improve the standards and practices of the profession.

However, the first real hospital, now St. Joseph's Hospital Health Center, did not open until 1869, after the Civil War. Today St. Joseph's is one of four medical centers in the area.

John Wilkinson is credited with opening the first law office in the village in 1820, although several attorneys had been practicing for years before that from offices in homes or other buildings outside the city. Hiscock & Barclay, which was started in 1855, is the oldest law firm still practicing today in the area.

Bond, Schoeneck & King, founded in 1897, has grown into the largest area law firm. Mackenzie Smith Lewis Michell and

Hughes, which started in 1884, is another major law office whose roots are deep in the Syracuse area.

The use of insurance spread gradually in the United States during the 1800s. Unity Mutual, which was started in 1903 by a fraternal order, is the oldest insurance firm based in Syracuse. The buying and selling of life insurance also spread slowly through the country. Today few Americans are without this protection for their families.

In 1830 businessmen saw a need and an opportunity and started a bank to fill that need and seize that opportunity. Today's bankers, insurance executives, and financial leaders are carrying on that tradition, enhancing and strengthening Syracuse's businesses, helping them grow, and providing jobs and a healthy economy for all.

This chef displays an appetizing spread at R.J. O'Toole's Restaurant in North Syracuse. Photo by David Revette Photography

Clinton Square is a peaceful oasis in a bustling city. Photo by Bob Mahoney

Chapter Seven

Shaping the Community
Planning, Development, and Real Estate

by Alexis O'Neill

During the 1950s Syracuse began to experience a phenomenon that also was affecting other urban areas: Americans on the move. Middle-class residents were on the move to the suburbs, retailers were on the move from downtown to outlying shopping malls, and city office tenants were on the move to campus-style office parks.

On one hand this movement from the city outward had positive effects, for it helped to develop attractive communities throughout the Greater Syracuse region and to bring services to convenient locations for suburban consumers. On the other hand this movement caused the Heart of New York to skip a beat: downtown Syracuse began to lose its vitality. Since the downtown area was widely regarded as a symbol of the region's economic, educational, and cultural strength, many believed that in order to inspire confidence in Greater Syracuse it was important to concentrate on rebuilding a thriving, active downtown. As a result, a variety of groups worked together to analyze the challenges Syracuse was facing in the 1950s and 1960s. They deliberately tried to play a role in determining how the city and the community at large were to take shape.

Two leaders emerged from that era with "bricks-and-mortar" reputations: William F. Walsh, who was mayor of Syracuse from 1961 to 1969, and John H. Mulroy, the first county executive in Onondaga County's history, who took office in 1962 and remained there until 1987.

During the Walsh years downtown

center, and underground parking for 100 cars. Called "a superb office building" by area critics, the renovated landmark, now known as the Clinton Exchange, is said to have inspired other renovations in the area.

Many houses and apartment buildings throughout the city also have been restored. The restorers have retained original architectural features while adding modern conveniences. In the historic Hawley neighborhood, row houses once owned by Greenway Brewery have become charming, sophisticated townhouses. One of James Street's oldest surviving mansions, Newell House, has been transformed from a condemned structure into an appealing office building by Newell House Partners. Built by carriage-maker Joseph Newell in 1872, this Second Empire style house was distinguished by a steeply sloping mansard roof. It was the residence of former Syracuse Mayor Thomas Ryan between 1907 and 1921. Preservationist Jay King, who has restored many houses and apartment buildings on the city's northeast side, headed the successful rehabilitation project.

Nettleton Commons, on East Willow and State streets, is one of the latest housing options in downtown Syracuse. It was originally the Nettleton Shoe Factory, and portions of the building date from 1884. Five additions had been made through 1922. Understandably, the developers, the Edgewater Companies, had to overcome many obstacles while converting the building into rental, retail, and commercial space. The outcome features Syracuse's first loft-style apartments, with enough windows and light to afford panoramic views of downtown Syracuse and the North Side. One- and two-bedroom units are also among the 61 spacious apartments. With close proximity to downtown and major highways, and the charming appearance of restored brick and wood, Nettleton Commons demonstrates a new use for industrial space that is both practical and pleasing.

Another attention-getting renovation project has been undertaken by the Franklin Square Associates, a subsidiary of The Pyramid Companies. Plans call for converting the Rescue Mission Alliance building on

Old buildings are frequently renovated into new office buildings. Photo by Oliver McConnell Photography, Inc.

Franklin Street and the New Process Gear plant on Plum Street into condominiums and office space. This is considered to be the first step in an ambitious plan for developing the lakefront of Onondaga Lake.

In addition to the rejuvenation of downtown, there has been almost unprecedented activity in new industrial and office parks, housing, and retail and commercial development.

OFFICE AND INDUSTRIAL PARKS

One of the most sought-after locations for recent commercial development in Onondaga County has been at Enterprise Parkway, between Bridge Street and Shoppingtown Mall. In the 1970s the area was largely ignored, and its soil was excavated primarily to provide fill for the construction of Interstate 690. Only a few years ago the land sold for $20,000 an acre. The price tag is double to quadruple that today.

In 1975 developer Joseph Scuderi of the Pyramid Brokerage Company, Inc., constructed an office building and called it "Widewaters" after a nearby section of the old Erie Canal. Widewaters Park is now a 70-acre development which consists of seven Class A office buildings. Two more are in the works. The Widewaters Group, which was one of the first developers in Syracuse to construct office buildings on speculation, has been successful in its gamble. Tenants include Agway, General Foods, and Metropolitan Life Insurance. Along the outer areas of Widewaters Park are such diverse companies as WIXT-TV, Medical Diagnostic Resources, Robson & Woese Engineers, Health Care Data Systems, the Touchette Corporation, and State Farm Insurance. Not far away on Towpath Road is developer Jack Rooney's site for Towpath Commons, a group of nine office buildings designed for professionals and small businesses.

Location is said to be the key to Enterprise Parkway's success: it is close to Routes 690 and 481, the restaurants and shops along Erie Boulevard, and some of Syracuse's top suburban communities.

The trend in the 1950s was to construct architectural business boxes with little thought given to landscaping or providing employee amenities. Today developers are more sensitive to the importance of creating total work environments that are both functional and aesthetically gratifying. Syracuse's industrial and business parks reflect this new attitude.

It is reflected in the 6.4-acre location for the engineering firm of Blasland, Bouck & Lee, Inc., on Towpath Road. Their 30,000-square-foot, high-tech building, constructed by Glacier Creek Development Corporation, incorporates 2.4 acres of designated wetlands into its landscaping design. Three ponds will preserve the character of the area. The DeWitt area will support another cluster of offices: the Pioneer Business Park developed by Michael Falcone of the Pioneer Development Company, which also developed downtown's One Park Place on Fayette Park. Pioneer Business Park is slated to include up to 13 office buildings at a site on Chrysler Drive, east of Carrier Circle. Amenities will include a restaurant, a fitness center, and the first day-care center in a privately owned office park in Onondaga County.

Salina Meadows, a corporate park developed by Rowe Development Company, constructed by Hayner-Hoyt Corporation, and managed by the John Lynch Company, is situated on 80 landscaped acres in Liverpool and features a jogging trail. Radisson Corporate Park to the northwest is part of a community with a master plan. On a large, appealingly landscaped site, one finds the corporate park, manufacturing and light industrial businesses, and recreational and residential facilities.

The quality, location, and attractiveness of spaces found in the Syracuse area may account for the high occupancy rates for Class A (top-of-the-line) office areas: 97 percent in downtown Syracuse and 86 percent in the suburbs, compared with national figures of 85 percent downtown and 78 percent in the suburbs. Prime office space in the Greater Syracuse area costs 30 to 50 percent less than it does in most metropolitan areas.

One reason given for why more companies are locating corporate headquarters and large branches in Syracuse is the continuing development of Hancock International Airport. Hancock, a major link in Greater Syracuse's unique transportation network, has grown from only 3 major carriers to approximately a dozen commercial and private lines in the last 25 years. The construction of a parking garage, undertaken at the urging of the chamber, has created protection from the elements for cars, an option applauded by the increasingly large numbers

Syracuse University is one of the
key educational institutions in
the city. Photo by Charlene Faris

Chapter Eight

Serving Diverse Needs

Education, Medicine, and Human Services

by Alexis O'Neill

J anuary 17, 1889, 8:45 a.m.: Crowds lined the streets around St. Mary's Circle. The spectacle was going to be too good to miss. Principal John H. Wilson paced in the lower corridor of the old Putnam School. Would it work? One by one, 17 classes lined up at the doorways. With arms laden with paper, inkwells, maps, books, and wastepaper baskets, children waited for the signal. At 9:00 a.m., the march began. Two by two, students stepped into the corridors—oldest first, youngest last—and onto the street outside. With Principal Wilson leading the way, a river of rosy-cheeked youngsters flowed from the doors of the old Putnam School on the corner of Montgomery and Jefferson streets to the new Putnam School on the corner of Cedar and Mulberry streets. When the seniors reached the new halls, the littlest ones were just leaving the classrooms that had seen 50 years of service. A giggle or two bubbled up as the children passed admiring throngs of adults. By 10:00 a.m. the move had been completed; students were bent over their textbooks, teachers were at the chalkboards, and the principal was on duty in the Syracuse City School District's newest building.

Doubters among the curbside spectators were silenced by this demonstration of what could be accomplished through organization, cooperation, and the willingness of each person to carry part of the burden. The greater goal was worth the planning effort— the goal of providing the best facilities possible to support and encourage the pursuit of knowledge, so that each student might have

cally for seventh and eighth graders who are at risk. Through this program, students benefit from a competency-based curriculum which focuses on motivation and personal attention. In addition, a developmental curriculum has been designed to accommodate children at the kindergarten level. Responsive to each child's specific cognitive, social, emotional, and physical time schedules, it allows children to pass from one level to the next at their own rates. High school students who choose a technical track attend classes at Central Tech located in downtown Syracuse. Those in the college program can accumulate advanced credits through a cooperative program with any one of the 25 colleges and universities within a 20-mile radius of Syracuse.

For enrichment, students participate in sports, art, music, drama, and a variety of other special interest clubs. From Shake-

speare in the park to the Scholastic Arts Festival, the Imagination Celebration, and the Jazz Festival, the talents of local students have many forums.

Each of the suburban districts maintains high academic standards, reflected in high grade-point averages, high SAT scores, National Merit Scholarship winners, and students who are successful in pursuing college or technical educations. In addition to the Syracuse School District, the local school districts include the Baldwinsville, East Syracuse-Minoa, Fabius-Pompey, Fayetteville-Manlius, Jamesville-DeWitt, Jordan-Elbridge, LaFayette, Liverpool, Lyncourt, Marcellus, Cicero-North Syracuse, Onondaga, Skaneateles, Solvay, Tully, West Genesee, and Westhill districts.

A friendly competition exists among districts in academic and extracurricular areas; when students compete in Onondaga

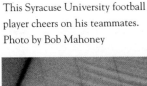

This Syracuse University football player cheers on his teammates. Photo by Bob Mahoney

County, they are often pitted against the best in the state if not in the nation. The West Genesee lacrosse team, recent winner of the state championship, went undefeated for years. Fayetteville-Manlius has earned distinction in soccer, and Liverpool has earned distinction in swimming. The Cicero-North Syracuse Northstars won the titles of Reserve Grand National Champions and AAA Champions of the Marching Bands of America Competition in Michigan after winning the New York State Championship at the Carrier Dome. The West Genesee Wildcats and the Liverpool Warriors marching bands also placed in the top five in the nation—a triumph for Onondaga County.

The Board of Cooperative Educational Services (BOCES) is a cooperative in its provision of instructional, technical, and management services and instructional resources. Many occupational education programs are available to high school students, including horticulture, computer electronics, printing, automotive engine rebuilding, electricity, and food service management. One division of the BOCES Adult Education Division is Skill Training for Employment (STEP), where training is offered in 20 fields. Included is training in the fields of business, electronics, food service, and nursing. More than 300 casual programs are also available through this division.

There are many programs within the Syracuse area that are cooperative efforts between industry and local agencies. A landmark vocational training project supports a score of technical education programs which provide students with specific skills in demand by local employers, ranging from word processing to weld-fitting.

In the early 1970s Greater Syracuse played an important role in a revolution in teacher education—a revolution based on the beliefs that a teacher's education continues throughout his or her professional career and that teachers' involvement in the development and implementation of programs is crucial to the success of the programs. In a cooperative agreement with Syracuse University, two teaching centers were established: one in the West Genesee School District, the other in the Jamesville-DeWitt School District. Teachers planned, taught, and attended in-service courses based on topics identified by the teachers themselves, and Syracuse University provided faculty

members and other resources in exchange for the placement and supervision of pre-service teachers.

To measure the success of the teacher centers, one only has to know that teacher centers were funded nationally during the Carter administration and that the New York State Education Department has funded teacher centers statewide since 1984. In addition to the two pioneering centers, the Syracuse Teacher Center serves Syracuse School District teachers, and the Central New York Teaching Center serves teachers in a consortium of 17 school districts in Onondaga and Madison counties.

For families that prefer schools outside the public system, the largest religious educational enterprise in the Syracuse area is the parochial school system of the Roman Catholic Diocese of Syracuse. Almost half of the diocese's elementary and secondary schools are located in Onondaga County. A variety of other private schools, including Manlius Pebble Hill, Max Gilbert Hebrew Academy, Montessori Discovery Elementary School, and Faith Heritage School, offer educational alternatives.

DAY CARE

Approximately 11,000 working women in the Syracuse area have children under age six. Unlike the 1950s, when 50 percent of American families had one parent at home full time, today only 6 percent do. Child care has become a major issue. In Central New York, parents, social service agencies, governments, and employers are attempting to work cooperatively to find the best solutions to the challenge of child care.

Several companies in Central New York have been cited for their innovative child care benefits. Among them are Fay's Drugs and MONY Financial Services. MONY, for example, offers employees the option of working an extra half-hour each day in exchange for every 10th day off to spend with family; the company has also developed a job-sharing program. The Syracuse School District has not only begun a job-sharing program but has developed a day-care program for employees' children: the Little Apples Child Care Center in Blodgett School on the city's near west side.

Other firms in Syracuse offering on- or near-site child care include the SUNY Health Science Center, James Square Child

These kids take time out to play at the fountain at Clinton Square. Photo by Oliver McConnell

The vastness of Syracuse's agricultural sector is seen here.
Photo by Dan Vecchio

Chapter Nine

Living Well
A Four Season Lifestyle

by Alexis O'Neill

There is something about Syracuse that when you come here, you know you've come home. No matter where you're from. No matter how long you stay.

As one woman from Eastern Europe said:

I had been used to big cities ... When my husband's work brought him here 30 years ago, I thought, "What will I do?" And then I went to a conference, and when I came back, I was going past where Columbus Bakery is. It was summer—the wonderful aroma of bread wafted into the window of my car and I thought, "Ah! That's home!" I found that this is one place where you absolutely can't say there's nothing to do. There are too many choices. And in minutes, you're out of the city into countryside. It's beautiful.

People born here sense it. People who move here know it. Syracuse has a distinct atmosphere—a special climate that makes this place interesting, civilized, livable. Some call it "quality of life."

Dr. Joseph Golden, Executive Director of the Cultural Resources Council of Syracuse and Onondaga County, writes:

One of the hallmarks of a vital and sophisticated community is the way it demands a certain quality of life... I think it means having choices; options; knowing that you can find what you need (emotionally or physically) in your own city. It means knowing that there are resources out there of all kinds—commercial, cultural, recreational, educational, religious, medical—of a quality high enough to make us feel secure and confident about finding the kind of protection and fulfillment that we need for a satisfying life.

What makes living in Greater Syracuse so satisfying? Some say it begins with the refreshing four-season climate. Some are proud of Syracuse's place in history as a port of call on the great Erie Canal. Some like the look of the region—the grand old buildings, wondrous new buildings, green parks, and refreshingly artistic public spaces that give it style and class. Others say it's the mixture of neighborhood feeling and big city opportunities that creates both a sense of belonging and a sense of excitement. Still others, with closets full of golf clubs, tennis rackets, bowling balls, fishing poles, and skis, bend ears about the area's recreational opportunities. And there are people who insist that it is the variety of top-notch visual and performing arts experiences, enjoyed by both viewers and participants, that gives this region an edge. To these features add colorful festivals, unique museums, distinctive shops, and top-notch restaurants. The result is

Greater Syracuse, an area with more than something for everyone.

THE FOUR SEASON LIFESTYLE

To smell the rich, dark soil turned and ready for planting; to see apple blossoms softening the hills of LaFayette; to hear streams rushing through the forests; and to feel the green freshness of the air is to experience spring in Central New York. Each season rewards the senses: the wraparound warmth of sunny summer days, the leaf-crisping days of autumn, and the crystalline white of brilliant winter days.

This four-season climate has inspired a variety of lifestyles and cultures, which give the community its strength and stability, and make it a desirable place to live, work, and play.

The temperature in Syracuse ranges from an average of 24 degrees in January to an average of 71 degrees in July. In the summer and autumn months, temperatures rise rapidly during the day but drop rapidly after sunset, providing nights that are cool and comfortable for sleeping. Skiers take advantage of the region's average snowfall of 110

Fountains and parks add to the city's beauty. Photo by Oliver McConnell Photography, Inc.

The Carrier Dome is a Syracuse landmark. Photo by David Revette Photography

inches, while farmers and water sports enthusiasts appreciate the average monthly rainfall of 3 inches, which is enough precipitation to comfortably meet the needs of agricultural and other water users.

So what's this about Syracuse being in the Snow Belt? Is it true? Yes. And there are those who could skip over winter and never miss it. Roads do get snowy, skies do get gray, and not everyone owns skis. But it boils down to what people are willing to endure for the season they like best. So they come. And they stay for generations.

For reasons not fully understood, the Greater Syracuse region attracts one of the most representative selections of Americans in the country. Historically Syracuse has been among the leading test markets in the United States, and residents have participated in countless accurate and successful new product tests for a variety of goods and services. Dancer, Fitzgerald, Sample (NYC), respected industry-wide as an authority on test marketing, ranks Syracuse third nationally. The city is credited with being one of eight cities with demographic characteristics projectable to the entire nation. Blue Chip corporations that have recently tested in Syracuse include Thomas J. Lipton, AT&T,

Campbell Soup Company, General Foods, Kellogg Company, Hills Brothers Coffee, and Coca Cola Foods. This shows that Syracusans have a sense of taste. It's been evident all along that they also have a sense of style.

A DISTINCTIVE LOOK

When a city delights, astonishes, stirs and inspires; when sound, light, and color stoke the spirit; when noise of a fountain is at least as strong as the noise of a truck; remarkable things happen to the psyche of citizens. They begin to like the place. Maybe even love it. And they're a lot more eager to sustain and protect it.
—Dr. Joseph Golden
Pollyanna in the Brierpatch

Fountains, monuments, parks, public art, and unique buildings make a walk through the City of Syracuse a treat and a drive through the region a sightseer's adventure. Limestone, cobblestone, brick, and frame constructions tell stories of skill of architects and builders as diverse as Archimedes Russell and I.M. Pei. They also reflect the other people and events that shaped the community, and the pride that local citizens take in

Cross-country ski trails are numerous in the Syracuse area. Photo by John Dowling

great northern pike, tiger muskie, panfish, bullhead, and channel cat. From 21-mile long Oneida Lake to crystalline Skaneateles Lake and the scenic waterways that stretch to the St. Lawrence Seaway and the Thousand Islands, the area is a paradise for boaters. More than 110,000 recreational boats lock through the canal system each year.

During the snowy months skiers enjoy four prime downhill slopes: Labrador Mountain in Truxton, Song Mountain in Tully, Toggenburg in Tully, and Greek Peak in Virgil. Three are within 25 minutes of Syracuse, and one is only an hour away. Cross-country trails abound in such places as Drumlins, Green Lakes State Park, Beaver Lake Nature Center, Highland Forest, Onondaga Lake Park, and Pratts Falls Park. Others also enjoy the snow: snowmobilers, tobogganers, and snowshoers all pray for a good season of those little white flakes.

For those who like to participate in organized leagues, the City of Syracuse Department of Parks and Recreation has many from which to choose: softball, with more than 350 teams; basketball, with 100 teams; and volleyball, with more than 60 teams.

THE PERFORMING ARTS

Picture a string of young boys scrambling after Buffalo Bill's open coach in Hanover Square, a crush of people filling the Weiting Opera House to hear Charles Dickens read from his works, or Sarah Bernhardt performing *Camille.* That was Syracuse in the 1800s.

For more than a century Syracuse has been a true cultural center—one which not only supports world-class arts organizations, but nurtures local talents.

At a recent Carnegie Hall performance, the Syracuse Symphony Orchestra was honored by a standing ovation and excellent reviews from New York City critics. One of only 32 major symphonies in the country, Syracuse Symphony has grown under the recent direction of Maestro Christopher Keene and the current direction of Maestro Kazuyoshi Akiyama. Concerts are performed in the Crouse-Hinds Concert Theatre of the Mulroy Civic Center, where solos by such renowned artists as Shlomo Mintz and Janor Starker have been performed. In addition to major concerts, a variety of outreach programs bring Symphony members in contact with the public throughout the region.

Since 1974 Syracuse Opera has brought

Upwards of 50 public and private golf courses, more than are found in any other area in the Northeast, are located in the city and outlying areas. An event that is anticipated eagerly each year is the Greater Syracuse MONY Classic Senior Pro Golf Tournament. The crowds lining the course at LaFayette attest to the popularity of the sport in this region.

When summer heats up, water events are in. Fishermen are lured to Onondaga County's 18 trout waters as well as to nearby rivers and streams which offer bass, walleye,

Beaver Lake is a haven for
wildlife. Photo by Dan Vecchio

WTVH-5

The year 1988 marks 40 years of service to the Central New York community by WTVH, Channel 5, Syracuse. Throughout four decades WTVH has been regarded as an innovative leader in the broadcast community and has achieved many historic braodcast firsts.

When WTVH-5 signed on the air on December 1, 1948, as WHEN-TV, Channel 8, it was the Syracuse area's first television station, and only the 47th station in the United States.

WTVH also was the first television property of Meredith Corp., a Midwest-based *Fortune* 500 company that publishes *Better Homes and Gardens*, *Metropolitan Home*, *Country Home*, *Successful Farming*, *Ladies' Home Journal*, and many other periodicals and books. Meredith remains the owner of WTVH and other television stations in leading markets nationwide.

Because WTVH went on the air before network television was fully operational, many of its early programs were local and live. Early programs included a series on how to fly an airplane, cooking shows, and "Fashions at Noon" from the Hotel Syracuse.

A CBS television network affiliate, Syracuse's WTVH presents a combination of strong local and syndicated programming from its James Street Studios.

In 1949 WTVH presented the first election returns seen on local television. Coverage of the political scene continues today with live debates by candidates, investigative reports and specials, plus complete election-night coverage.

Remote broadcasts, now fairly common, were a general practice at TV5 in its early days. Many other television stations were not capable of remote broadcasting until the late 1970s. WTVH reintroduced local live coverage of news events during the 1976 elections when its "Live Eye" microwave remote camera unit premiered.

During the early 1950s the station

WTVH anchors Ron Curtis and Maureen Green are part of an award-winning news team that has made "Newscenter5" Central New York's most popular source of news.

introduced "The Magic Toy Shop," a station-produced children's program that preceded CBS' "Captain Kangaroo" by six months, as well as other network-produced children's television programs. "Magic Toy Shop" left the air in 1976, but the children's program continued as "Toy Shop Corporation," making it one of the longest-running programs for young children in television history. Thousands of young Central New York adults remember "Magic Toy Shop" as an integral part of childhood.

In 1962 the FCC assigned Channel 5 to the station in order to make additional channels available in Central New York. In 1976 the FCC approved WTVH as the station's new call letters after Meredith sold a sister AM radio station along with its WHEN call letters.

WTVH has had a commitment to community involvement and service since its sign-on. The station makes airtime available for many public service and community projects.

The station was one of the founders of the community's Winterfest, and promotes warm-weather events of the Cultural Resources Council, Onondaga County Parks and Recreation Department, and other community groups as part of the annual Summerfest.

"Mass for Shut-Ins" has brought religious services to those unable to attend church; it began in WTVH's pioneer days. And minority groups find program time available, giving them a voice in the community.

Recently WTVH has focused on community needs through telethons to support the Syracuse Symphony, to build a new county zoo, to raise funds to send local high school bands to national competitions, to raise dollars to support black colleges, and to provide funding for research and health care for foundations fighting disease.

The station also has assisted Literacy Volunteers to obtain recognition for the organization and attract volunteers to teach reading to adults who are unable to read. In 1984, when the unemployment rate in Central New York was at its highest, WTVH devoted an entire evening to a Job-A-Thon designed to match jobs at area employers with residents seeking work.

Jean Daugherty, WTVH's public affairs director who has been with the station since 1950, is a Syracuse institution. She has devoted most of her adult life to producing more than 15,000 documentaries and public affairs programs for TV5. Among her recent efforts was "Something Special," an award-winning documentary series that monthly focuses on the unique quality of life in Central New York.

"Newscenter5," the centerpiece of WTVH's local programming, is Central New York's most popular source of news. Ron Curtis, veteran newscaster and anchor of "Newscenter5," along with its award-winning news team, are the dominant force in local news. In addition to strong local coverage, "Newscenter5" has broadcast live news remotes from the Middle East, New York City, New Orleans, and Los Angeles, as well as from nearby cities. News specials, reflecting events that impact the local community, are aired even while the events are happening, making "Newscenter5" the equal of any news operation in the country today.

Affiliated with the CBS television network since its early days, WTVH presents a combination of strong local and syndicated programs, which enables the station to maintain a dominant role in Central New York broadcasting and advertising.

Now in its fifth decade of operation, WTVH stands firmly behind a commitment for continued community service to the Central New York area. The management and the 100-member staff of WTVH believe they have an obligation to help make Syracuse and Central New York a better place to live and work. Growth and prosperity for the community are viewed as essentials for the continued success of the station.

THE WIDEWATERS GROUP

The corporate offices of The Widewaters Group give three distinct impressions. The first is one of prestige created by an eclectic blend of marble, imported hardwoods, original artwork, and muted shades of grey and mauve. The second is one of quiet efficiency; the third denotes detailed planning and organization.

Combined, these three impressions represent the essence of The Widewaters Group, developer of more than one million square feet of first-class suburban office space in the Syracuse, Rochester, and Albany areas of New York State.

The Widewaters Group, whose headquarters is in Widewaters Office Park, the company's signature development in DeWitt, just east of Syracuse, has experienced unprecedented growth. This growth is based on a philosophy of developing and maintaining ownership and complete active management of all its projects.

This approach—complete and continuous control over all facets of its real estate developments—is made possible by an extensive organization of

Widewaters VI Office Building, The Widewaters Group's signature development and the firm's headquarters in Dewitt, New York.

in-house capabilities. These include architectural and interior design, construction, and property management, even to having the company's own janitorial firm. This control results in unsurpassed quality of services to tenants on a daily basis.

Joseph T. Scuderi, The Widewaters Group general partner, started the venture in 1981 after many years of experience in development work as a partner in other firms in the industry. One of the company's first projects was the 1982 rehabilitation of Nixon Gear Building, an industrial plant that was converted into a multitenant office facility.

In 1982 Scuderi also began work on the company's first building in Widewaters Office Park, a 30,000-square-foot facility. The office park, situated on 65 acres near the geographic center of New York State, is representative of the suburban office parks the corporation has developed and main-

tains. The name comes from a wide stretch of the Erie Canal portion that once flowed through the area.

Widewaters Park is a unique interplay of buildings and natural open spaces. The development blends the best urban characteristics with the lush and extensive landscaping of a suburban campus. Each building is carefully

The conference room in The Widewaters Group's suite of offices reflects the design and decorating details that have become a company trademark.

located within its own designated space to ensure balance and harmony. Trees, grass, foliage, walks, and courtyards abound.

Parking is ample and close to each structure. Still, each parking area is concealed discreetly by natural screens to maintain the park's visual integrity.

Today seven buildings have been completed in Widewaters Park—each unique, but bearing a relationship to its neighbors. Each is characterized by the expert use of exceptionally high-quality materials and workmanship. Oak predominates throughout each. Lobby areas feature balcony/atrium designs with skylights, extensive plantings and seating areas. Lobby floors are quarry tiled; walls combine oak, brick, and glass. The attention to detail and service that exemplifies Widewaters Park is indicative of the company's attitude toward its other developments in the Upstate region of New York.

Woodcliff Office Park, located in suburban Rochester, is one of the first multiuse projects in the area. The 264-acre site features an office park, a residential community, a resort, and a conference center. When completed, Woodcliff will contain seven office buildings.

Woodcliff I, which opened in 1986, is a 76,000-square-foot, multitenant office building that typifies the high standards of design and workmanship of all The Widewaters Group properties. Woodcliff I provides companies with a unique business environment offering tenants special advantages found in no other office complex in the area—the opportunity to work, live, and relax in one location.

To that end the Woodcliff Residential Community features a mix of 450 condominiums, town houses, and single-family homes, plus the Sports Club, a recreational facility adjacent to tennis courts, a swimming pool, and a golf course. These features combine to

Corporate Woods II, an office building in Liverpool, New York, developed by The Widewaters Group. The firm maintains ownership and complete active management as with all of its projects.

form a total life-style concept unique in the Rochester area.

The Lodge at Woodcliff was designed for the needs of business travelers. This multistory hotel includes conference and banquet facilities for up to 300 people, four mini-units with kitchens, and 250 guest rooms, plus a restaurant and coffee shop—all in a country setting of rolling hills, winding trails, and breathtaking seasonal foliage.

Apart from its suburban office developments, The Widewaters Group has been instrumental in the renovation of numerous industrial buildings throughout the Syracuse region. The firm's renovation projects and office parks are credited, in part, for the emergence of Syracuse as a viable business center.

In 1988 The Widewaters Group entered retail development by beginning construction of Roseland Center, a 180,000-square-foot shopping center in Canandaigua, New York. The company also controls hundreds of acres for potential office sites and malls in many parts of the Upstate New York region.

Since 1981 The Widewaters Group's innovative approach to office building construction and maintenance, and its renovation of existing commercial and industrial facilities into first-class, state-of-the-art office

It is always springtime in the lobby of Woodcliff I, a Widewaters Group development in suburban Rochester. The office park is adjacent to the Woodcliff Residential Community, providing the opportunity to work, live, and play in one community.

space have created a standard of excellence unsurpassed in the development field. The quality, efficiency, and organization readily apparent in the company's corporate offices are impressive. Most important, these same impressions are imparted by every project that The Widewaters Group undertakes.

Chapter Thirteen

Manufacturing

Producing goods for individuals and industry, manufacturing firms provide employment for many Syracuse area residents.

Courtesy, Carrier Corporation

trucks, containers, fishing vessels, and ships' stores.

Carrier is among the world leaders in transportation air conditioning and refrigeration. Equipment designed, engineered, and manufactured by Carrier Transicold Division makes possible the shipping of fresh and frozen foods worldwide; the safe transport of medical supplies such as blood plasma and lifesaving pharmaceuticals; and the transport of other materials and products whose temperature and humidity must be maintained at specified levels.

Carrier Corporation also leads the industry in product coverage, offering more than 350 product lines in some 23,000 configurations. The firm operates the air conditioning industry's most advanced residential and commercial product development and testing facilities, including five international primary design centers that focus on improving and differentiating the company's residential and commercial air conditioning products. It also operates several international design modification centers, which alter new Carrier products to meet local market requirements.

The organization's 500 graduate engineers around the world are linked by a computer network that enables all to share in technology and advanced product development ideas. Carrier en-

Hermetic compressors march down the assembly line at Carrier's Carlyle Compressor Company facility in Syracuse. The compressor is often described as the "heart" of an air conditioning system, and Carrier devotes much of its engineering efforts toward improvements in compression technology.

gineers work on dozens of sophisticated projects related to new materials and components, as well as products and complete systems. These projects revolve around a core of four critical technologies: compression, heat transfer, electronics, and air management.

Research is focusing on new designs for compressors, the heart of the air conditioning system; on new concepts to reduce further the size and cost of heat exchangers and other products; and on improving operating efficiency.

Electronics is playing an increasingly important role in the control of equipment. Carrier engineers are continuing to apply electronics to improve equipment performance, energy efficiency, and reliability, as well as to more quickly and accurately diagnose equipment problems and manage building systems with a supervisor computer.

Syracuse also is the headquarters for several Carrier units, including Carrier Transicold; Carlyle Compressor Company; Latin American Operations; and Replacement Components Division, which markets replacement parts and components for the industry.

Other Carrier units are situated strategically around the world, enabling the corporation to produce equipment close to its customers and to meet competition from companies in other nations as well as domestic firms.

The Syracuse-based organization has the biggest share of the world's largest air conditioning market, the United States, where approximately 40 percent of all the air conditioning equipment is sold. Carrier also leads in sales in South

Carrier Transicold container refrigeration units near completion in Carrier's Syracuse Building TR-20. Container units help assure the safe transport of fresh and frozen foodstuffs and other perishables throughout the world. In 1987 the company received the largest single order in its history—a contract to provide more than $20-million worth of container units that will cool bananas being shipped from Latin America.

and Central America, and has a strong presence in Europe, the Middle East, and Asia-Pacific markets, giving the firm its worldwide sales leadership.

Carrier residential heating and

A rooftop air conditioning unit is readied for testing in Carrier's Commercial Products Laboratory in Syracuse. Rooftop units provide heating and cooling in structures such as shopping centers, schools, and small office complexes. The facility evaluates the units' abilities to withstand various climatic conditions as well as vibrations encountered in shipping.

cooling systems continue to make an impact on where and how people live. By controlling indoor temperature and humidity, even in the driest desert or dampest jungle, Carrier residential cooling systems have helped to open entire new regions to housing development, from the U.S. Sun Belt to Saudi Arabia. In colder climes modern, compact furnaces, incorporating microprocessors, deliver uniform heat efficiently and quietly.

Carrier heat pumps provide optimum heating and cooling, and a new generation of heat pumps incorporates a system for domestic water heating. Carrier electronic air cleaners remove dust, pollen, and other pollutants from air, and central system humidifiers keep air moisture at proper, comfortable levels.

As markets for air conditioning continue to shift, Carrier plans to change its focus and goals to meet these changes, as it has done throughout the 1970s and 1980s.

In recent years Carrier has expanded its product design, manufacturing, purchasing, and marketing capabilities—particularly in developing countries—to win new customers for its products. The firm also has expanded its worldwide market penetration by acquiring or establishing joint ventures with nearly 60 companies in 28 countries from Latin America to the People's Republic of China.

Carrier's objective with acquisitions and joint ventures has been to establish global prominence in the industry. The onset of offshore competition, namely Japanese manufacturers, and the growth of markets outside the United States required this aggressive strategy.

What Willis Carrier perceived that foggy night in 1902 was a principle that had been apparent for centuries—clues could have been found by anyone who saw drops of moisture that had condensed on a cold window or a container of cold beverage.

Still, that principle went unrecognized until the young engineer realized what it meant: Cold air holds less water than hot air. Therefore, it should be

possible to control humidity in air by cooling it.

Controlling humidity was Carrier's immediate objective. He had been hired by a Brooklyn printing company to find a way to reduce the humidity that was causing problems with color registration. In summer, colors printed on dry days would not register (line up) with those laid down on warm, humid days when the paper absorbed moisture and expanded.

Carrier devised an apparatus that passed air over chilled coils. There the moisture condensed, reducing its humidity before the air was sent to the press area. The young inventor found, too, that he could control the humidity precisely by varying the temperature in the coils. He also discovered that the drier air was cooler, and so he could control the temperature as well as the humidity.

Carrier had sufficient vision to realize that his invention held a greater future than just controlling humidity. Cooler air meant more working comfort, and cooling retail stores, theaters, and other buildings meant more customers in warm weather.

Carrier created the first air conditioner—a device that passed moist air through a chamber saturated with water vapor—while at Buffalo Forge, where he had convinced executives to allow him to set up a research division

To ensure reliability, Carrier tortures its equipment in environmental test labs such as these. This Carrier heat pump coated with ice is forced to defrost itself repeatedly in conditions more severe than anything it is likely to encounter in regular service.

Improving air conditioning efficiency through new heat exchanger technology is a never-ending challenge. The performance of each new heat exchange surface is evaluated in Carrier's Central Engineering Services test loop in Syracuse.

with himself as the only employee.

Carrier Corporation moved to Syracuse in 1937—brought to the city as part of a program to revitalize manufacturing and overcome the effect of the Great Depression. Today Syracuse still is home to the company.

Carrier intends to continue its aggressive manufacturing and marketing strategies to maintain its global leadership in the industry—whose annual new equipment sales approaches $20 billion. As this market develops, Carrier Corporation intends to be there, leading the way with the best products and the best people, as the Syracuse firm has done throughout the first air conditioned century.

Everybody still talks about the weather. Willis Carrier finally did something about it. His company is continuing to improve on what he started.

B.G. SULZLE INC.

B.G. Sulzle Inc. is the largest independent surgical suturing needle manufacturer in the world today. In its factory on Northern Lights Circle, Sulzle produces more than 2,000 different types of needles used in all types of surgery.

Sulzle needles are known worldwide, as the highest-quality suturing needles available to the medical profession. The firm produces them for use in every operating procedure employed by the medical profession—from tiny needles the thickness of three human hairs to large needles used to place "stay" sutures, which hold a previously sutured incision or wound together.

For years Sulzle needles have been used in most open-heart and transplant operations in the United States. The Syracuse company's hand-honed line of small-size needles for plastic surgery are used in most emergency rooms throughout the United States.

Starting in 1945, Sulzle has produced needles for suture manufacturers around the world. The organization is now the primary supplier for firms in Europe, North Africa, the Middle East, Southeast Asia, Australia, Japan, Korea, and South America, as well as being the major independent supplier for suture manufacturers in the United States.

The firm's reputation rests on a special kind of needle designed in 1945 by the company's founder, Benjamin G. Sulzle. His revolutionary design was for a needle that has a hole drilled laterally in its end, rather than an eye as most surgical needles had.

Sulzle customers insert a suture in the hole, crimp the end on machines manufactured by Sulzle, then package, sterilize, and distribute the needle/suture product to hospitals. Sulzle itself makes only the needles and crimping machines.

Founder Ben Sulzle's idea of drilling a hole into the end of the needle was not easy to put into production, and involved the design of the entire needle production line. His design,

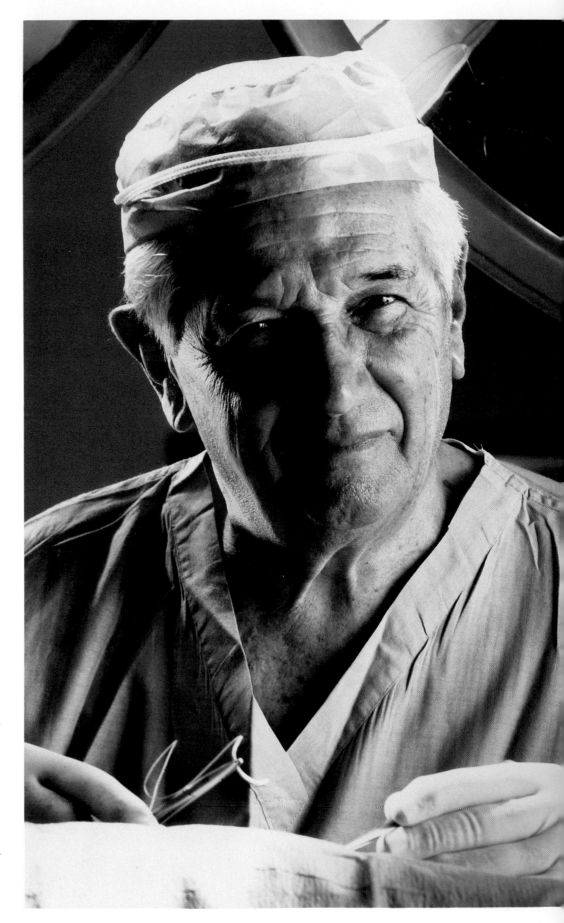

Dr. Ernest L. Sarason uses sutures with Sulzle needles during an operation.

however, today is still the basis for Sulzle's business. Production of the needles has been updated to bring the plant into the computer age.

The smallest needles made by Sulzle use a drill that is exactly the thickness of a human hair. It is used on a suture that is a single extrusion of the silkworm, and is so fine that it will float away in normal air conditioning if it is not held in place.

One of Sulzle's foremost achievements was the design of the diamond point needle, a trademarked needle with a small spatula-like point that will slip through layers of tissue with almost no resistance. This needle, which has a slim blade-cutting area, allows the surgeon to pick up small layers of tissue without disturbing the area surrounding the suture line.

As the firm moves into the final decade of the twentieth century, Sulzle plans to expand its sales areas even further, particularly in South America and the third world countries of Asia and Africa.

A Sulzle drilled-end, diamond-point surgical needle.

Many doctors in these regions have been trained in the United States and Europe to use the highly specialized needles that Sulzle provides to the medical profession. When these physicians return to their own countries, they demand the same high-quality products they have trained with.

B.J. Sulzle Inc. is still a family-owned and -operated firm, part of Syracuse's new wave of high-technology manufacturing companies that provide highly specialized products to world markets.

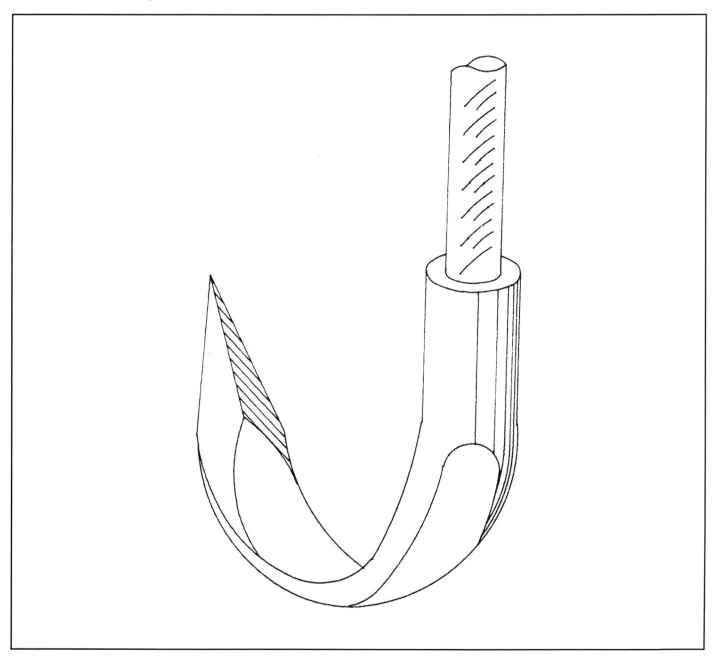

SYRACUSE CHINA CORPORATION

Syracuse China Corporation, which traces its roots to a small pottery established in suburban Syracuse in 1841, today is the leading and largest U.S. manufacturer of commercial dinnerware for the food-service industry. The organization not only produces and markets more open-stock patterns but also makes and sells more custom-design china than any other company in the United States.

Today Syracuse China dinnerware is used in a wide range of food-service operations—from contemporary "in" dining places to the finest hotels, and from industrial caterers to schools, clubs, resorts, and institutions nationwide.

The company has concentrated on manufacturing commercial dinnerware for the hotel and restaurant industries since 1971. It has been a major supplier of commercial dinnerware since 1896, when it introduced the rolled-edge design—the first china created specifically to withstand the heavy usage of commercial dining establishments.

The rolled edge became a worldwide standard for commercial and institutional food service, and the firm quickly captured a major share of that market.

It still maintains that lead, principally due to the millions of dollars Syracuse China has invested in computerized equipment and data-processing systems to modernize manufacturing operations and achieve maximum efficiency and productivity. Computers, for example, control precisely the mixing of ingredients for each batch of clay, and sophisticated equipment handles forming, decorating, and other processes.

Manufacturing technology and systems are being refined continuously at Syracuse China, allowing the company to compete better and continue to produce the dinnerware that sets world standards for style, beauty, and durability. Skilled craftsmanship continues to play a major role in maintaining the traditional beauty and durability of its dinnerware, as well as the rich heritage of innovation associated with the firm for more than a

century.

Two other major achievements followed the rolled edge during the next decade. In 1897 decalcomania was introduced, and the company became the first American pottery to set up a ceramic lithographic printing operation using multicolored decals for overglaze china patterns.

In 1908 the corporation announced a major breakthrough in china decorating: underglaze decalcomania, a technique that applies a clear glaze protection over multicolor china patterns to preserve the designs for the life of the ware. Syracuse China was the first dinnerware with this protection.

In succeeding decades the company introduced many new dinnerware styles, patterns, and shapes for the home and commercial establishments. Included were Airlite, the first china designed for airline dining; Syralite, a whiter, thinner, and lighter china made with alumina, a white bauxite material; and dinnerware designed specifically for tables in railroad dining cars.

The organization officially dates its beginning in 1871, when 13 stockholders purchased the Empire Pottery operation—which traced its roots to W. H. Farrar's 1841 pottery—and reorganized as Onondaga Pottery Company.

In 1890 Onondaga Pottery realized a major long-sought-after goal: production of a fully vitrified china, the first made in the United States. This china was white, thin, and translucent dinnerware, and stronger than those made in Europe. The new china, the first to carry the Syracuse China backstamp, won a medal of honor at the 1893 Columbian Exposition. This achievement and others that followed earned for Syracuse China a wide reputation for excellence and innovation.

Sales and production expanded as demand grew nationwide. In 1921 the company built a new plant on Court Street and transferred commercial dinnerware production there. Consumer dinnerware production continued in the West Fayette Street plant. The

Court Street facility, now the firm's only Syracuse factory, has been expanded several times. Today it encloses more than a half-million square feet of space.

After weathering the Great Depression and World War II the organization continued expanding sales with new styles and shapes as well as decorating innovations.

One of Syracuse China's elegant patterns for the food-service industry.

Five generations of family owner-ship ended in 1971, when the company became a public corporation. The new management immediately focused on meeting higher demand from the grow-ing multibillion-dollar food-service industry, spurred by Americans' in-creasing appetite for away-from-home dining. That trend continues, fueled by more varied cuisines and the entry of more women in the work force. Syra-cuse China discontinued production of consumer dinnerware that year.

Currently Syracuse China Corpo-ration operates the Syracuse plant and three others: Syracuse China of Can-ada in Joliette, Quebec; Mayer China in Beaver Falls, Pennsylvania; and Shenango China in New Castle, Penn-sylvania.

In 1978 Syracuse China share-holders voted to merge with Canadian Pacific Enterprises (U.S.) Inc., the Syracuse-based U.S. subsidiary of Canadian Pacific Ltd., one of Canada's largest firms. As a subsidiary of CP, Syr-acuse China Corporation has retained its identity and management, and pos-sesses the resources to meet confidently the challenges of the future.

CRUCIBLE SPECIALTY METALS

Crucible Specialty Metals is a part of Crucible Materials Corp., a new company with a historic past and a bright future.

Crucible Materials Corp. (CMC) became a privately held independent corporation on December 20, 1985, when the Crucible divisions were purchased from Colt Industries by an employee group. CMC, with headquarters in Syracuse, includes plants in Georgia, Illinois, Kentucky, Pennsylvania, Wisconsin, and Sheffield, England.

Syracuse-based Crucible Specialty Metals Division, CMC's largest unit with more than 1,400 employees, combines state-of-the-art techniques with the latest equipment and know-how to produce the finest specialty steels in the industry. Specialty Metals' principal products include high-alloy and high-speed steels and stainless steel, plus the proprietary CPM (Crucible Particle Metallurgy) steels. Most products are shipped as bars, rods, or wire.

Steels made by Crucible are used for tools in the metalworking, automotive, appliance, woodworking, and other industries; for jet engine bearings; for automobile and truck valves; and in marine items, nuclear reactor components, and other high-performance applications. These products are sold through 14 service centers nationwide, which stock, cut, and deliver steel orders in all the U.S. metalworking markets.

The company employs two basic melting methods: the electric arc fur-

Located just west of Syracuse, the Crucible plant extends more than 65 acres in area. The site was originally occupied by Halcomb Steel in 1902.

nace, which was first used in the Western Hemisphere at the Syracuse mill in 1906 for conventionally produced steels, and the induction furnace, which produces CPM steel.

Conventional arc melting uses high-grade scrap and alloys, which are melted and refined to precise chemical specifications and then rolled, drawn,

Molten steel is poured into Crucible's 40-ton argon oxygen decarburization vessel for further refinement to the precise chemical composition of specialty metal.

or machined to finished form.

In the CPM process, which also was first used commercially at Syracuse, molten pre-alloyed steel is atomized into minute particles, which are screened and compacted to a density of 100 percent. Subsequent finishing operations are the same as with conventional steels. The internal soundness of CPM steel gives it superior performance capabilities in use. Crucible is the only domestic source of CPM steel.

The division's complex on 65 acres west of Syracuse houses two electric arc furnaces (40- and 22-ton), a two-ton air-induction furnace, a 40-ton argon-oxygen decarburizer, 2,000-pound forging press, bar mills, heat-treating and annealing furnaces, wire mill, and other equipment to make top-quality steels.

Crucible's history began in 1776 in Sheffield, England, with a steel-making partnership, Naylor and Sanderson. Later the firm became Sanderson Brothers & Co. In 1876 Sanderson launched a crucible-melting steel plant in Syracuse. Sanderson and other steel firms merged in 1900 to form the Crucible Steel Co. of America.

In 1911 the Halcomb Steel Co., organized in 1902 by C.H. Halcomb, also was acquired by Crucible. The two Syracuse mills were combined as the Sanderson-Halcomb Works in 1946. The company became Crucible Specialty Metals in 1968.

L. & J.G. STICKLEY, INC.

Stickley recognized since 1900 for the beauty and enduring quality of its handcrafted furniture, today remains committed to one goal: producing the finest solid wood furniture in the United States.

That commitment started with the company's founders—Leopold Stickley and his brother, John George—and is continued and enhanced by Alfred Audi and his wife, Aminy, who purchased the company in 1974. The Audis have revitalized the firm and maintained its reputation for producing the finest and best-made furniture.

Stickley craftsmen still make the furniture painstakingly by hand, one piece at a time, each signed and dated by a proud cabinetmaker. Younger workers learn their skills from longtime craftsmen, some of whom worked with Leopold Stickley, acknowledged by many as the revered dean of American cabinetmakers.

Over the years Stickley manufactured solid oak, maple, and cherry furniture. In the early 1900s the company's Mission Oak line was purchased for its utilitarian function as well as for what it represented in life-style. Furniture collectors today prize the Mission pieces, as well as the cherry furniture Stickley specialized in after World War I.

The firm recently added a formal line of mahogany to its traditional cherry offerings.

With its legendary reputation for the finest construction and the most translucent finish, as well as its timeless and elegant designs, demand for Stickley's bedroom, dining room, occasional, and executive office furniture continues to grow rapidly.

By 1988 Stickley's sales exceeded $20 million annually—10 times the $229,000 in sales in 1974 when the Audis purchased the ailing company from Leopold Stickley's widow, Louise, who had owned the firm since her husband's death.

Alfred Audi has known and admired Stickley furniture since childhood and later through his association with E.J. Audi, the family's store in New York City.

After 85 years in Fayetteville, Stickley moved into a larger, one-floor plant in the neighboring Syracuse suburb of Manlius in July 1985. The new building doubled manufacturing capacity as well as increasing efficiency and productivity. Another expansion in 1987 increased its total space to 200,000 square feet.

Stickley furniture is sold nationwide through a very select dealer network. In addition, the firm has showrooms in Rochester and Albany, as well as in its Manlius headquarters building. Cherished and esteemed by connoisseurs and collectors nationwide, every Stickley piece bespeaks art as well as utility.

Alfred and Aminy Audi, owners of L. & J.G. Stickley, Inc., outside the plant entrance that reflects the company's commitment to produce the finest in solid wood furniture.

The finishing room staff at Stickley.

IBM

IBM, a corporation whose initials are probably the best-known business identification in the world, has been in Syracuse since 1917. That Syracuse office opened only six years after three diverse companies merged in 1911 to form the Computing-Tabulating-Recording Company, the forerunner of today's International Business Machines Corporation.

Thomas J. Watson, Sr., became president of CTR in 1915 and began to mold it into a firm that embodied his character and beliefs. Three of those beliefs have become very basic to IBM, and the adherence to them has been the key to its success. Respect for the individual, offering the best-possible customer service, and the pursuit of excellence have helped IBM become one of the most admired and successful companies in the world.

In 1924 CTR became the International Business Machines Corporation, and under the leadership of Watson, continued to grow. As an alternative to laying off factory workers during the Great Depression, when nearly one-quarter of the work force was unemployed, Watson instead chose to expand by building IBM's parts inventory. That choice paid off in 1935, when Congress passed the Social Security Act. IBM was selected to undertake one of the greatest bookkeeping operations ever. Because they maintained such a great supply of parts, they were able to build machines, and begin delivering their products at once.

In its early years CTR marketed such products as butcher scales, meat slicers, coffee grinders, time clocks, and punch card tabulating machines. Today IBM's current product line ranges from office typewriters to personal computers, to mid-range and mainframe computer systems.

The latest addition to its mid-range family of products is the IBM AS/400 System. This new system consists of a broad range of compatible processors, which provide an easy growth path for diverse environments in businesses of all sizes. The AS/400 is designed for ease of operation, and features extensive menu prompts, built-in- on-line education, and electronic customer support, which provides automatic problem determination.

IBM has grown into a worldwide leader in developing, marketing, and servicing a broad range of information processing products and systems like the AS/400. Its operations are worldwide, including manufacturing and marketing organizations in Europe, the Far East, the Mid-East, and Australia.

Locally CTR opened a Syracuse service office in 1917 in the Unity Mutual Life Insurance Company building at 628 South Warren Street, where the Red Cross Building now stands. Later two sales divisions were added—the International Time Recording Division and the Tabulating Division, which sold sorters and accounting machines. A typewriter division was opened in the 1930s.

In 1949 IBM relocated its operations to 529 South Warren Street, a location chosen personally by Watson during a visit to Syracuse. By 1959 IBM's Syracuse operations had grown into a district office and education center for employees and customers, and the company again moved.

That time IBM relocated its operations to two buildings at 973 and 1000 James Street. Housed in the buildings were a field systems support center, a data center, a data-processing sales office, and a field engineering service office.

Today more than 300 IBM em-

IBM's move to this Warren Street location in 1949 was initiated by company president Thomas Watson, Sr., during a visit to Syracuse.

ployees occupy four floors in One Park Place on South State Street in downtown Syracuse, where the firm moved its operations in 1983 when the new building opened. The space houses a U.S. Marketing and Services Group sales office, a National Service Division office, a parts distribution center, and a customer center that displays IBM equipment and provides customer training.

Through the years IBM has not only provided products and services for its customers, but also has offered sup-

Advisory marketing support representative Bob McGraw conducts an Expert Systems Seminar in the IBM Customer Center.

IBM's management staff resides on JA's board of directors, and assists with the recruiting of new businesses to participate in the Junior Achievement program.

IBM also supported the New York State Special Olympics by lending equipment and technical assistance, along with the time and talents of employee volunteers.

Over the years IBM has developed a unique partnership with the local business community and the City of Syracuse. As a partner with companies of every size, from banking, insurance, and government, to education, health, and retailing, and as a partner in local community involvement, IBM is working in Syracuse for the continued growth and success of the entire Central New York area.

port to local communities as well.

The IBM Employee Charitable Contribution Campaign is an annual solicitation of employees for contributions to the United Way and other locally approved agencies. Through payroll deductions IBM employees can make donations to the charities of their choice. This has proven to be an effective way of funding the services required by local communities.

Here in Syracuse IBM employees have made annual contributions to many United Way agencies and charities, such as the United Way of Central New York, the American Cancer Society, and the American Heart Association.

IBM is also a major business sponsor for the Junior Achievement of Central New York. Company volunteers spend time with area high school students, helping them develop and manage their own miniature corporations. In addition a representative from

Systems engineer Rebecca Logan displays the new IBM AS/400 system.

GENERAL SUPER PLATING COMPANY, INC.

A sign on the wall in the office of Herbert N. "Duff" Gerhardt, Jr., president of General Super Plating Company, Inc., says: "When you're through changing, you're through."

That statement is a declaration of General Super Plating's philosophy. GSP has changed almost constantly since 1964, and continues to change to meet the demands of its customers.

By following that philosophy, the DeWitt-based, privately owned firm has grown to become the largest plastic plater in the East, and one of the largest and most modern in the United States. It maintains that position, despite a disastrous 1979 fire that destroyed its main plant just outside Syracuse and forced the company to rise from the ashes like a modern phoenix.

And, as the use of plastics increases in all industries—particularly in electronics—GSP expects business to continue to grow. "Our growth since 1966 has almost all come from the plastics industry," says Gerhardt.

GSP is one of the fewer than 20 plastics plating companies in the United States. Orders for plating plastics come from numerous companies in the electronics industry, including many *Fortune* 500 firms, and provide GSP's largest single volume of business. The second-largest volume of orders comes from the automotive industry.

The firm uses the latest processes, including proprietary processes developed by its research and engineering staffs, for plating plastics and other work in its four divisions. Much of the firm's production machinery and

The automated plastic plating line. General Super Plating is one of the largest plastic plating companies in the United States.

equipment are custom-made for GSP.

GSP's four divisions, which occupy more than 100,000 square feet of space in four buildings, are Plating on Plastics; Metal Finishing; Adhesives, which applies adhesives to bond automotive and other parts; and the Shielding Division, which provides EMI/RFI shielding for business machine enclosures. The Shielding Division moved into a new plant on Joy Road in June 1987 to better accommodate the growing need for this service.

After a disastrous fire in 1979 General Super Plating Company was rebuilt and production resumed the following year.

The organization was founded in 1932 in a three-car garage by W.A. Phillips and Herbert Gerhardt, Sr. Both worked at a silver plating company and decided to moonlight by doing chromium plating in the evenings. Phillips eventually left his job to devote his energies to the plating operation on a full-time basis. Gerhardt soon joined him.

In 1964 the Gerhardts acquired Phillips' interest and became full owners. Metal plating was the company's main business in 1964, and employment totaled 37 people.

Two years later the firm entered the new field of plating on plastics. Gerhardt's decision to begin plating plastics accelerated the company's growth—a growth that continues. GSP currently employs more than 250 people.

Today the company is truly a family-owned and -managed firm: Gerhardt's son, Thomas, manages two divisions; his son-in-law, Scott Greenleaf, is vice-president; and his daughter, Kim Greenleaf, is administrative director.

After the 1979 fire the Gerhardts decided to rebuild in the same location, with the help of financing through industrial revenue bonds issued by the Onondaga County Industrial Development Agency. Limited production resumed in early 1980, and later that year General Super Plating Company, Inc., again was plating plastics and metals at full capacity.

JAQUITH INDUSTRIES

Jaquith Industries, Inc., is a specialized metal fabricator whose experience and expertise make the Syracuse company a leader in the manufacture of airport equipment, metal forms for concrete forming work, and custom contract fabrication for a variety of products ranging from boat anchors to commercial laundry machines.

Skilled workers with many years of experience team up with Jaquith's completely equipped production facilities to fabricate metal bars, plates, sheets, and tubes into a broad variety of cost-effective products that serve the needs of diverse markets worldwide.

Each of Jaquith's three manufacturing specialties—Vega® Airport Equipment, BMF® Metal Forms, and Custom Contract Fabrication products—was developed as the company anticipated and responded to emerging trends in commercial, industrial, and military technology, notes Donald S. Jaquith, president and owner since 1976.

For many years Jaquith has been the leading supplier of airfield lighting hardware, consisting of in-runway and edge-marker light bases and transformer housings, adapters, covers, and base plates. Its aluminum and fiberglass breakaway approach lighting masts, designed and manufactured to withstand adverse environmental conditions, meet Federal Aviation Administration and international standards for safety.

Jaquith's products are found in airports in Europe, the Middle East, Asia, Africa, and North and South America, including such well-known fields as JFK, O'Hare, Dallas-Fort Worth, London's Heathrow, Jeddah International, and the Kennedy Space Center.

Locally, Jaquith supplied all the hardware for the recent Hancock International Airport runway rebuilding project. The company's high-strength BMF® forms helped mold the poured-concrete median barriers on Interstate 81, as well as I-690 and other area highways.

Jaquith's Custom Fabrication Department makes many of the outer shells and stainless-steel cylinders for the G.A. Braun Inc.'s industrial laun-

Jaquith products are marketed in many countries worldwide.

dry machines, as well as specialized weldments for other local industries.

The dedication and experience of Jaquith's 100-plus work force is especially important because many of Jaquith's products are related to safety—median barriers for safer driving, run-

Jaquith airport lighting products and breakaway lighting masts help make safer takeoffs and landings.

way lighting for safer takeoffs and landings, and anchors for safer mooring.

Jaquith Industries' ability to deliver on time, and often ahead of schedule—whether for government contracts, exports, or special orders—was proven effectively when the National Aeronautics and Space Administration sought specialized lighting equipment for the space shuttle program. The Syracuse company developed and produced hardware for the shuttle's alternative landing sites within a turnaround time of 15 working days.

BRISTOL-MYERS COMPANY

Bristol-Myers Company's Industrial Division, headquartered in Syracuse, is an international affiliate of the *Fortune* 500 company. The division serves as the manufacturing arm of the Bristol-Myers Science and Technology Group, producing many of the firm's pharmaceutical products, including anti-infective and anticancer agents.

Beyond this primary duty, however, the Industrial Division is also responsible for the development of manufacturing processes for new pharmaceutical compounds discovered by the research unit of the Science and Technology Group—the Pharmaceutical Research and Development Division.

The Pharmaceutical Research and Development Division, headquartered in Wallingford, Connecticut, conducts basic research in the company's major therapeutic areas: anticancer, central nervous system, cardiovascular, anti-infective, and dermatology.

At the same time, other research division groups in Seattle, Washington, are taking Bristol-Myers into areas that make the organization a part of the bio-medical advances expected to dominate drug discovery and therapy in the early part of the twenty-first century.

Bristol-Myers' presence in Syracuse dates back to the early 1940s, when the company purchased Cheplin Biological Laboratories in order to produce the then-new wonder drug, penicillin, as part of the World War II effort. Over the years the Syracuse complex has continued to expand. While the production of penicillin still is a major enterprise, the plant on Thompson Road also manufactures other broad-spectrum antibiotics.

In addition to its manufacturing responsibilities, process development plays a very significant role in the division's mission. The division's Biotechnology and Chemical Development centers at the Syracuse location are state-of-the-art facilities that study and develop new and better processes for the manufacture of pharmaceutical

Fermentation of antibiotics and other manufacturing processes are controlled by computers from this control room.

products. There the technologies of genetics, biochemistry, biotechnical engineering, chemistry, and chemical engineering are employed in developing these processes.

In the years ahead the Production Division also is preparing to enhance its role in the application of newer technologies, such as molecular biology and

An aerial view of Bristol-Myers Industrial Division's 53-building manufacturing-research complex in Syracuse, which fronts on Thompson Road (the lower diagonal highway).

New compounds found by Bristol-Myers research units worldwide are sent to the Industrial Division's pilot manufacturing plants to determine if the compounds can be produced efficiently and in commercial quantities. Pilot plants, such as this one, also work to improve manufacturing of current products.

genetic engineering, that are expected to increase the use of biological processes in the manufacture of the pharmaceuticals of the future.

Techniques that Bristol-Myers Industrial Division scientists will employ will include growing mammalian cells instead of microorganisms for use in producing therapeutic agents. These techniques will use the same principle as growing bacteria to produce antibiotics such as penicillin, but they will be for new purposes and different kinds of therapeutics.

The Biotechnology and Chemical Development Center plays an integral role in what president T. John Potter calls his division's foremost goal: manufacturing the highest-quality products possible at the lowest cost.

As noted, the Industrial Division is an international business unit. Overseas locales include manufacturing facilities in Latina, Italy; Barceloneta and Mayaguez, Puerto Rico; and Santo Domingo, Dominican Republic.

The finished pharmaceuticals produced by the Industrial Division's plants are marketed domestically by the Bristol-Myers U.S. Pharmaceutical and Nutritional Group, and worldwide by the Bristol-Myers International Group.

As a supplement to these efforts, the Industrial Division itself sells bulk antibiotics on a worldwide basis to those who want access to the company's high-quality products.

In addition to its manufacturing and development capabilities, the Industrial Division also is home to the

firm's Central Engineering Department. This unit is responsible for the design and construction of Bristol-Myers facilities worldwide, as well as providing other forms of related consultation expertise.

Bristol-Myers Company, which celebrated its first century in business in 1987, currently employs 35,000 professionals worldwide, providing consumers with health care, beauty care, household products, and technology that help to enhance and prolong people's lives.

Other Industrial Division research focuses on biotechnology and genetic engineering, using such tools as these X rays of the DNA (deoxyribonucleic acid) chain. Bristol-Myers believes biotechnology and genetic engineering will play major roles in developing future pharmaceutic agents.

Robson & Woese, Inc., 208

Bond, Schoeneck & King, 214-215

The Young Agency Inc./Royal Insurance Company, 223

Greater Syracuse Chamber of Commerce, 209

O'Brien & Gere Limited, 216-217

Mackenzie Smith Lewis Mitchell & Hughes, 224

Key Bank of Central New York, 210-211

Sargent Webster Crenshaw & Folley, 218-219

The Galson Companies, 225

Onbank, 212

Continental Information Systems Corporation, 220-221

Paul J. Cowley & Associates Advertising/Marketing/ Public Relations, 226

Hiscock & Barclay, 213

GTE, 222

Chapter Fourteen

Business
And
Professions

Greater Syracuse's professional community brings a wealth of service, ability, and insight to the area.

Courtesy, Oliver McConnell

PAUL J. COWLEY & ASSOCIATES
ADVERTISING/MARKETING/PUBLIC RELATIONS

Opposites attract success at Paul J. Cowley & Associates. The agency influences the future for its clients, but lives in a piece of the city's past—a turn-of-the-century red-brick home. Inside, creativity comes first, but it's played off the wall of reality.

The results are both striking and effective.

Opposition had a role in the agency's beginning as well. Early in his studies Paul Cowley rejected a teacher's judgment: "You're never going to make it in the field of art."

Believing in his abilities, Cowley moved to New York City, attended the School of Visual Arts, and gained agency experience. When he came back to Syracuse, he was ready and eager to light up his hometown with "Big City" energy. Syracuse, of course, had advertising agencies, but Cowley's enthusiasm and talent quickly found an appreciative audience.

At the first Syracuse Society of Advertising Arts Award Show in 1973, his work was honored with 30 prizes, including six awards given for television.

Encouraged, Cowley founded The Design Company in 1975. As talent drew talent and Cowley met more of his clients' needs, his agency grew. In 1979 it was incorporated as Paul J. Cowley & Associates Inc.

Today the firm employs 15 people and serves a roster of national, regional, and local clients. Still excelling in design, the agency has taken its "creative and effective" philosophy into print, radio, and television advertising; sales promotion; market research; media planning; and public relations.

"The best advertising solves a problem creatively," says president Cowley, and his work has done that for many local industries. An image campaign for Syracuse's G.A. Braun Inc. raised awareness of the firm's technological advances and helped lead to the highest sales in Braun's history.

Advertising for Eastern Microwave, a Syracuse-based common carrier serving the cable television industry, won the top print award for the 1985 CTAM (Cable Television Administration and Marketing Society) com-

petition and increased new affiliate contracts 25 percent in one year.

The Intelligent Alternative campaign for WRVO-FM, a National Public Radio affiliate in nearby Oswego, won an award from the Corporation for Public Broadcasting and added nearly 15,000 new members, while raising a year's development funds in just six months.

In 1984 design work for a local restaurant (with nothing more than the architect's drawings for reference) brought national advertising's most prestigious award: a Clio for U.S Package Design.

Another client who has enjoyed awards along with success is Learbury Clothing, a Syracuse menswear institution. Since retaining Cowley in 1983, Learbury's retail outlet at its Syracuse plant has shown annual sales gains of 40 percent.

Internationally, Cowley has prepared advertising for D.J. Giancola Exports Inc., targeting customers in the Caribbean and Latin America, and for Diagnostic Medical Instruments Inc. to promote its products in China.

National and international commercial efforts are balanced with community involvement. Cowley gave the City of Syracuse its slogan: We're the Heart of New York. Other agency work has benefited "Teen Talk," a radio counseling program reaching troubled youth, as well as the century-old Rescue Mission, the Hospice of Central New York, New Hope Pregnancy Aid Cen-

ter, Faith Heritage School, and many others.

"By working with clients and products we feel genuinely enthusiastic about, and doing good work for them, we've been successful," says Cowley. "As we add new people and new technologies, we're able to do more and more."

The newest addition is a computerized graphic design system that adds speed and versatility to the agency's proven design capability, a real plus for clients interested in logo art, corporate identity, and packaging.

Meetings of the old and new, imagination and brass tacks, and award-winning work that works in the marketplace are the past, present, and future of Paul J. Cowley & Associates.

Advertising Marketing Public Relations 315 N. Clinton St.   Syracuse, NY 13202 • Phone (315) 473-8453 • FAX (315) 473-8408

226

Coyne Textile Services,
242-243

Agway Inc., 244

Dairylea Cooperative Inc.,
245

New York Food Brokers Inc.,
246

Hotels At Syracuse Square,
247

Chapter Sixteen

The Marketplace

The area's retail establishments, service industries, and products are enjoyed by residents and visitors to the area.

Courtesy, Bob Mahoney

Index